CALIFORNIA
HIKING WITH KIDS

50 Hiking Adventures for Families

Bridge Press

Bridge Press

Support@BridgePress.org

ISBN: 978-1-955149-32-7

FREE BONUS

Find Out 31 Incredible Places You Can Visit Next! Just Go To:

purplelink.org/travel

TABLE OF CONTENTS

INTRODUCTION:
HIKING WITH KIDS

Welcome!

This book is your guide to the best hikes for kids in the great state of California. As the third largest state in America, California has a lot to offer in outdoor activities. With just about every type of terrain available, California's hikes are diverse with lots of animals, flowers, and artifacts.

Hiking is one of the best ways to get off electronics and active in nature. Hiking is also a great experience to share with family, as parents and children explore and discover the world around them and their own physical abilities. Hiking is also a great way to learn outside of the classroom in a more hands-on environment where learning about nature, maps, and science can be fun.

Strap on your hiking books, fill up your water bottle, and start planning your next family outing. The following pages are filled with great day hikes the entire family will love and talk about for years. Pick hikes in one specific area or try them all. Here are 50 hikes for kids in California.

Tips for Hiking with Kids:

Hiking can be a fun but strenuous activity. In order to make the time you spend on the trail enjoyable, a few essentials will make all the difference. It goes without saying that some of the items on this list are no-brainers, but some items may be new to you. If you are planning on becoming an avid hiker, these items will be a great investment.

The must-haves on every hike are: water, snacks, sunblock, hat, waterproof hiking boots, and a comfortable backpack. It's also great to use the bathroom before you hike, as some trails don't offer toilets. Some of the trails can be steep, rocky, or difficult, so it's always good to have a hiking buddy along to make sure everyone is getting through the trails safely. With so much to think about and learn, let's see what works best.

What to Bring:

Liquids:

Always have water on hand when you hike. Some of the best water bottles are the kind that will keep your water cool and refreshing. Water bottles made from glass protect against BPAs. Some bottles are collapsible for storage, and others will filter your water for you. All of these are great choices as well as whatever water bottle you are currently using. As long as it holds water, it's a good choice. Other liquids to bring are sports drinks with electrolytes to help you retain water. Also, citrus juices like orange juice will provide sodium and potassium.

Snacks:

You will get hungry. Small snacks are great while hiking so you won't feel tired from eating but will remain energized. Great snacks to bring are trail mix with dried fruits, seeds, granola, and nuts. For longer hikes, turkey jerky is a good source of protein for energy, as well as protein bars and snack bars. Fruit is a great and easily carried snack for the trail. All of these can be stored in your backpack. For shorter hikes, bring some sandwiches as well that you can enjoy when you reach the end of the trail. Most trails have a picnic area, and you can enjoy some relaxation and good food after your hike. A light weight, soft-sided cooler bag is great for storing items that may spoil in the heat.

Gear:

Desert and Southern California hikes: the climate in Southern California is very dry and indicative of summer. Many desert hikes provide zero shade from the sun, so for these hikes bring: hiking boots for the sand and rocks, sunscreen, hat, and sunglasses. Also good for these kinds of hikes is a backpack that includes a bladder. A bladder is a plastic sack that sits in your backpack that you can fill with water. The sack has a long straw that goes over your shoulder so that you can drink water whenever you need it. Wear light clothing like t-shirts and shorts to keep yourself cool.

Mountain hikes in Central and Northern California can be cooler and even snowy. For these hikes, wear long pants and sleeves, not only for temperatures but because these climates also have a lot of ticks. The mountains also tend to be wet, so waterproof shoes or water shoes are great to wear. Hiking sticks are also great for getting up the steep mountain inclines. For mountain hikes in the snow, goose down jackets are great, as are spikes that can go over the bottom of your shoes to grip into the icy and snowy terrain. Goggles are also a great item to have in the event that it is windy on the mountain top, and you need to prevent the sun and snow from getting into your eyes.

Shoes:

Toddlers: boots and shoes with great movement and flexible sole and traction

Kids: shoes with traction

Teens: hiking boots

Backpacks:

Toddlers: reflective, easy to clean, and lightweight

Kids: comfortable and padded with lots of storage and a water bladder

Teens: comfortable straps, lots of storage, ultralight with sternum strap

Best Hikes Breakdown:

Northern California

- Dave Moore Nature Trail
  - 1 mile, easy — Toddlers/Young Kids
- Stream Trail
  - 5.5 miles, moderate — Older Kids/Teenagers
- Cataract Falls Trail
  - 4.8 miles, moderate — Older Kids/Teenagers

Central California

- Valley View Trail
  - 1.8 miles, easy — Toddlers/Young Kids
- Vernal Falls
  - 4 miles, moderate — Young Kids/Teenagers
- Lower Mariposa Grove
  - 6.2 miles, moderate — Young Kids/Teenagers

Southern California

- Dana Point Headlands
  - 1 mile, easy — Toddlers/Young Kids
- Shipwreck Trail
  - 4.6 miles, moderate — Older Kids/Teenagers
- Santa Ynez Falls
  - 2.3 miles, moderate — Younger Kids/Teenagers

Best Desert Hikes

- Pictograph Trail
  - 2.6 miles, moderate — Older Kids/Teenagers
- The Cross Trail
  - 2.3 miles, moderate — Younger Kids/Teenagers
- Ladder Canyon
  - 4.4 miles, difficult — Older Kids/Teenagers

Best Mountain Hikes

- Prewett Point Trail
  - 0.7 miles, easy — Toddlers/Young Kids
- High Peaks/Bear Gulch Trail
  - 7.7 miles, difficult —Teenagers
- Chalone Peak Trail
  - 7.7 miles, difficult — Teenagers

ABOUT CALIFORNIA

California's topography offers a lot for those who seek to be active outdoors. Overall, California has a climate for pretty much anyone. From mountains to deserts to beaches and cliffs; if you are looking for a certain climate, California has it. California is flanked by mountains to the east and west. The Sierra Nevada Range is in the eastern part of the state, and the Tehachapi Mountains are in the southwest. There are also several soil-rich valleys like Napa and the Central Valley, with Death Valley, which is a desert, in the southeastern part of the state.

Landscape and Climate

- Northern California
  - Wildlife – typical of warm mild summers and cold snowy winters
  - Flora – redwoods, sugar bush, holly leaf cherry, desert willow, lilacs, sycamores, cottonwoods, gray pine
  - Fauna – snakes, sea lions, elephant seals, bighorn sheep, otters, wolves, deer elk, black bear, dolphins, and whales

- Central California
  - Wildlife – indigenous to a Mediterranean climate in the north and more desert climate in the south

- o Flora – oaks, grasslands, riparian forests, with freshwater marsh plants
- o Fauna – muskrats, black-tailed deer, blue herons, hawks, mule deer
- Southern California
  - o Wildlife – varies from oceanic to desert
  - o Flora – aloe vera, palm trees, cacti
  - o Fauna – coyotes, cougars, black bears, otters, hawks, racoons, weasels
- Mountains
  - o Wildlife – indigenous to higher elevations
  - o Flora – oak trees, white firs, and sugar pines
  - o Fauna – mountain chickadee, mule deer, grey squirrel, beavers, black bears, wolverines, golden trout, mountain lions, black bears, and the California mountain kingsnake
- Desert
  - o Wildlife – indigenous to extremely dry climates
  - o Flora – varieties of the Mojave yucca, Joshua tree, desert candle, and common saltbush
  - o Fauna – desert tortoise, black-tailed jack rabbit, turkey vulture, and coyote

Dave Moore Nature Trail, American River Parkway, Lotus, California

The Dave Moore Nature Trail is a one-mile loop trail that is very easy to hike and is best suited for small kids and toddlers. Dogs are allowed on the trail as long as they are on a leash. Bathrooms are not available near the trail.

There are small dinosaurs along the trail that children can take with them on the hike or move to other areas of the trail for other children to find. The trail is next to the American River, which was once home to the gold rush. Americans panned for gold in the 1800s.

Best time to visit: The trail is accessible all year round. Strollers and wheelchairs can only access a small portion of the trail.

Pass/permit/fees: It costs $5 to enter American River Parkway. The fee is increased to $8 on summer holidays.

How to get there: American River Parkway is located off of Interstate 80 at the State Highway 49 exit. Take highway 49 to the park.

What to pack: The Dave Moore Nature Trail is a short hike, but there is no water available in the area. Make sure your water bottle is full and there are some snacks for the kids like trail mix or jerky.

What can you find? Lots of nature can be found on this trail like rattlesnakes and bobcats as well as flora like black locust, gray pines, western sycamores, and larkspurs.

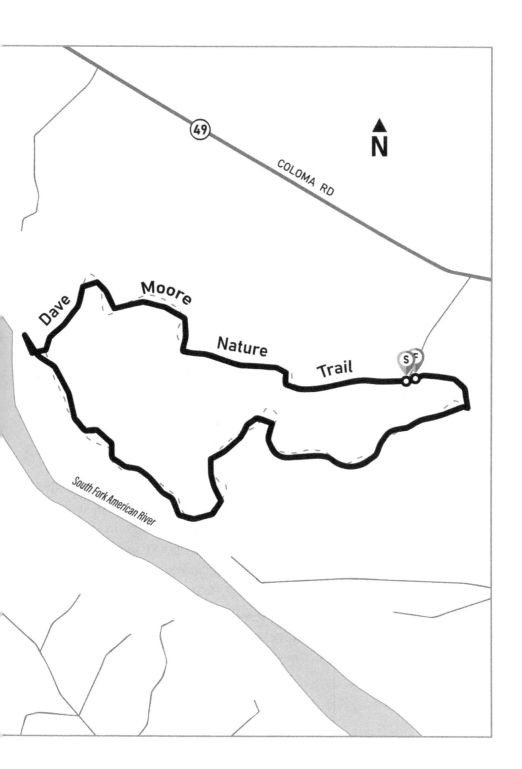

Subway Cave Trail, Lassen National Forest

The Subway Cave Trail is a .7-mile hike that is easy to do especially if you have toddlers and small children. The trail is inside a long cave that was once a viaduct for flowing lava and volcanic rock thousands of years ago. There are stairs on either side of the hike in order to make taking the trail a lot easier. Dogs are not allowed on this trail. Bathrooms are available. Parking is available.

Lassen National Forest was created about 20,000 years ago from cooled volcanic rock from the eruption of Lassen Peak.

Best time to visit: April through October

Pass/permit/fees: During the summer, it is $30 to enter Lassen National Forest. In the winter, it is $10. All permits are valid for seven days. There are six days during the year entrance is free. Visit their website for more detailed information.

How to get there: Lassen Park is located ¼ of a mile north of Old Station, CA, on highway 89.

What to pack: The inside of Subway Cave can get very chilly, so pack a light jacket. There is also no light in the cave, so make sure you have a flashlight on hand, too. The terrain is slightly rocky, so wear sturdy hiking shoes with good soles to prevent slips or ankle rolling. There is a picnic area after this short hike and packing a small picnic lunch is recommended.

What can you find? You may see raccoons, skunks, mule deer, chipmunks, and woodpeckers. Plant life in the area is comprised of ground cones and copper moss.

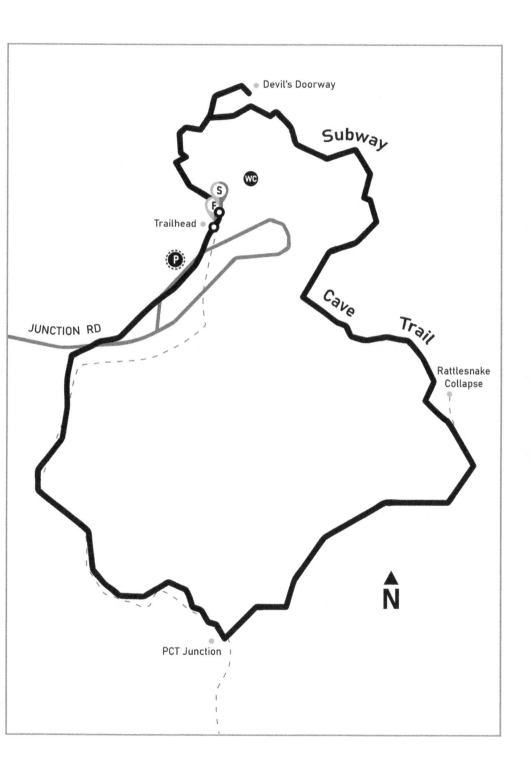

Devil's Doorway

Subway

WC

S

F

Trailhead

P

JUNCTION RD

Cave

Trail

Rattlesnake
Collapse

N

PCT Junction

13

Potem Falls Trail, Whiskeytown National Recreation Area

Potem Falls is a .4-mile hike. The easiness of the hike makes it great for toddlers and younger kids. The trail ends at the 69-foot tall Potem Falls that crash down into Lake Shasta. This trail is great for a stroll or walk. Dogs are welcome to use this trail.

Best time to visit: The trail is best used April through October.

Pass/permit/fees: It is $25 to enter Whiskeytown National Recreation Area.

How to get there: Whiskeytown National Recreation Area is located on State Highway 299. Take Interstate 5 to Highway 44 to Downtown Redding and hop on Highway 299.

What to pack: You can swim in the lake at the end of the trail, so bring some swim shorts or water shoes. Sunblock is also recommended. It's a short hike, so any kind of trail mix or jerky is a good idea — or sandwiches. There is no water on the trail, so a full water bottle is a necessity, as is bug spray for mosquitos. Wear good hiking shoes as the trail is rocky and uneven.

What can You find? Aside from the beauty of Lake Shasta, there are black bears, mountain lions, and coyotes. You'll see hummingbirds, ospreys, frogs, and snakes. There is an abundance of spring flowers as well as ponderosa pines and oak trees.

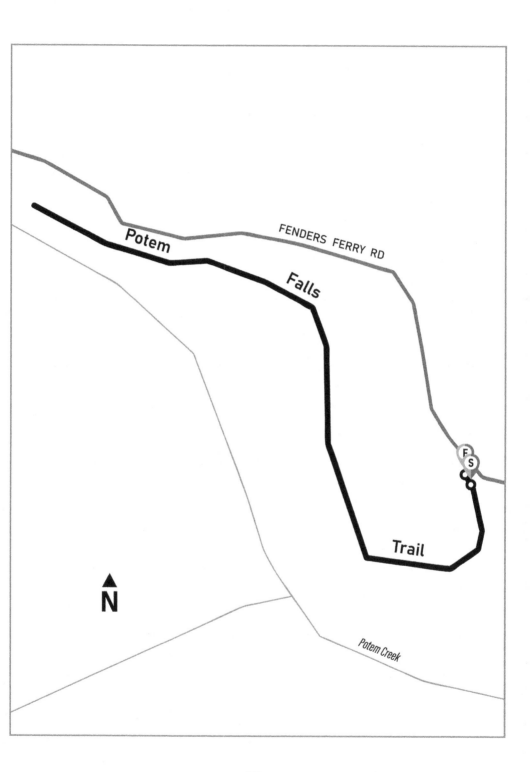

Patrick's Point Trail, Patrick's Point State Park

Patrick's Point State Park is 640 acres of land that sits on the edge of the Pacific Ocean. The Patrick's Point Trail is a very short .2-mile hike that offers beautiful views of the ocean. The hike is recommended for toddlers and small children, as it is a very short walk to a very beautiful scenic overlook. There are several trails in the park that intertwine with each other, so if you want to continue walking a bit further there is more for you to experience. Bathrooms are located near the visitor center, and most of the trails are not wheelchair or stroller accessible. Dogs are not allowed on the trails.

Best time to visit: The best time to experience Patrick's Point is April through October when there are clearer views and no fog.

Pass/permit/fees: It is $8 to enter Patrick's Point.

How to get there: Patrick's Point State Park is along California State Highway 101.

What to pack: Pack sunscreen and hats. Have sturdy hiking shoes as well in case you decide to try one of the other trails. Pack light snacks for the hike, but there are picnic areas by the visitor center if you choose to leave some food in the car for a picnic later. Bring binoculars for whale watching.

What can you find? During the spring and fall, you can see whales in the ocean during their migration period. There are also sea lions, seals, and black-tailed deer. Among wildflowers, you'll see fair

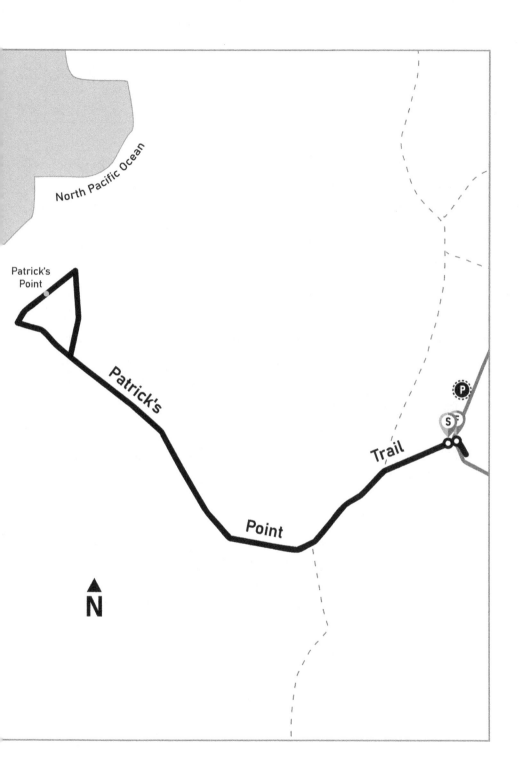

North Pacific Ocean

Patrick's
Point

Patrick's

Point

Trail

Fern Canyon Loop Trail, Prairie Creek, Redwoods State Park

Fern Canyon Loop is located in Redwoods State Park, which is home to the mighty redwood tree. The trail has several creek crossings and is home to a 50-foot canyon wall of ferns. The trail is a 1.1-mile, relatively easy trail that is good for younger kids to older kids. Some toddlers may find the trail fun. Bathrooms are not available at the trailhead.

Fern Canyon Loop was the location for the show *Walking with Dinosaurs* and the blockbuster film *Jurassic Park 2: Lost Worlds*.

Best time to visit: The trail is accessible all year round but is best enjoyed in spring and summer when the flowers are in bloom. The trail gets a lot of traffic, so try and go early.

Pass/permit/fees: It costs $8 to enter Prairie Creek, Redwoods State Park.

How to get there: The park is located on Highway 101. Access the Drury Scenic Parkway off of Highway 101 to access the trailhead.

What to pack: Bring sturdy hiking shoes and waterproof shoes for crossing the creek (the water is about ankle deep), sunscreen, hats, sunglasses, and a backpack of snacks. Bring a poncho in the event of rain. There is also beach camping available, so it may be worth packing some tents and sleeping bags if you are looking to camp for the night.

What can you find? There are five species of ferns in the park as well as redwood trees. You'll see frogs and centipedes among beavers and deer.

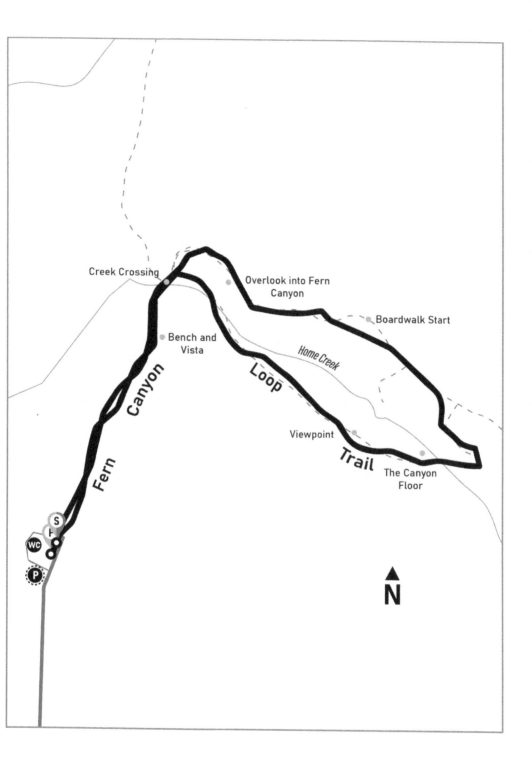

Creek Crossing

Overlook into Fern Canyon

Boardwalk Start

Bench and Vista

Home Creek

Fern Canyon Loop Trail

Viewpoint

The Canyon Floor

S
H
WC
P

N

Ney Springs and Faery Falls, Mt. Shasta

Ney Springs and Faery Falls are located on Mt. Shasta. The hike is about 1.5 miles long and is an in-and-back hike. The trail ends at Faery Falls and winds through what used to be the Ney Springs, which was a health resort. As you go on the hike, you will pass ruins of what used to be the buildings of the resort. This hike is good for younger kids to older kids, but some toddlers may be able to take the hike since it is short.

Dogs are allowed on this trail but must be kept on a leash. Bathrooms are not available near the trail.

Best time to visit: The trail is best used between May and October when the falls are at their full capacity. When visiting, go early, as the trail can get crowded and seeing the surrounding area may get difficult.

Pass/permit/fees: It is free to enter Mt. Shasta. Permits are required if you want to camp.

How to get there: Take Interstate 5 to exit 738. Once off the exit, use your GPS to guide you to the trail head, as there are a few twists and turns to make it to the mountain.

What to pack: The trail can get rocky, so bring sturdy hiking boots with ankle support. The terrain can also get a bit muddy. It's a short hike, so some light snacks and water are recommended.

What can you find? Hikers will be able to see the old ruins of Ney Springs Resort. The area is full of black bears, deer, prairie falcons, and red-tail hawks. As you are walking through the vegetation, you will see wildflowers, violets, and lilies.

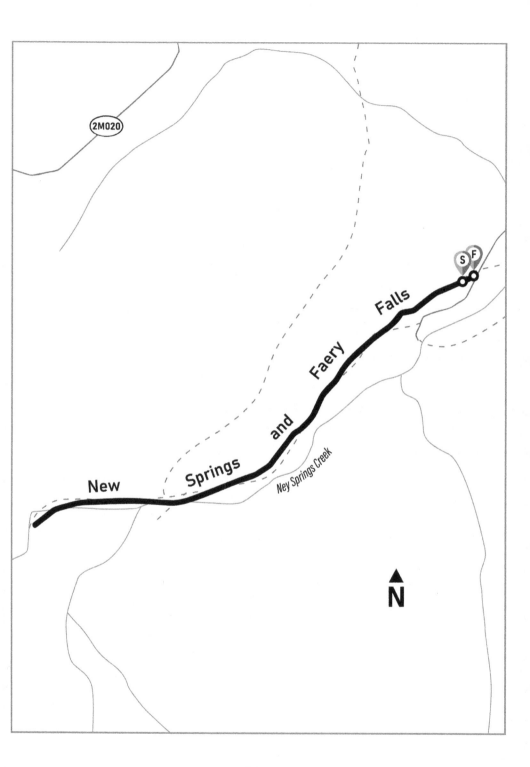

Big Nasty Trail, Lava Beds National Monument, Tulelake

Lava Beds National Monument was created after the volcanic explosion of the Medicine Lake volcano hundreds of thousands of years ago.

The trail is a 2.3-mile loop that should take about an hour to complete and is best suited for older kids and teenagers. Some younger kids may be able to take the trail in stride. Dogs are not allowed on this trail. Bathrooms are not available.

Best time to visit: Hiking on the trail is best suited between March and October.

Pass/permit/fees: It costs $25 to enter Lava Beds National Monument.

How to get there: Lava Beds National Monument is located on Hill Road off of Highway 161. Check your GPS for more detailed directions.

What to pack: Be careful of ticks. Long pants are recommended. Bring bug spray as well for mosquitos. The trail is long, so snacks like trail mix and jerky are a good choice, as well as a full water bottle. Bring a hat and sunscreen for sunny days.

What can you find? Mountain lions are often seen in Lava Beds National Monument, so be on the lookout. You'll also see bats, rattlesnakes, and kangaroo rats. The plant life features ponderosa pines and wildflowers.

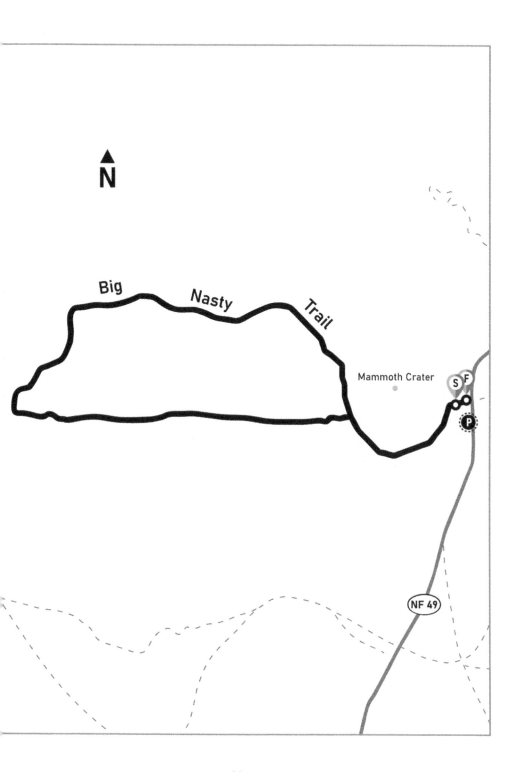

Stream Trail, Redwood Regional Park

The trail is a 5.5-mile hike. This trail is better suited for older kids and teenagers. The terrain can get slippery and muddy so being able to hike unassisted is a plus. Bathrooms are located at the several park entrances, but not by the trail.

Redwood Regional Park has the largest remaining natural strand of redwoods on the East Bay. During the building of San Francisco, the area was used as a logging site to chop down wood to build the city.

Best time to visit: The trail is accessible all year round, and it's best to get there early before it gets crowded.

Pass/permit/fees: It is $5 to enter the park plus $4 if you have a trailer. Dogs are charged $2. Fees are collected at the Redwood Gate entrance.

How to get there: Redwood Regional Park is located on Highway 13 in Oakland, California. You can take the mass transit BART system from Oakland to the park.

What to pack: Hiking boots for the water and the mud are a must. Bring bug spray for mosquitoes and ticks. The trail is long, so sandwiches that won't spoil are a good idea. Bring plenty of water.

What can you find? Redwood Regional Park is also the site of a pure strain of rainbow trout. A historic landmark (#970) is located in the park to help you identify where the trout are living. Fishing is not allowed in the park. There are also squirrels, golden eagles, deer, racoons, and rabbits. Plant life along the trail are grasslands, evergreens, and the mighty redwood.

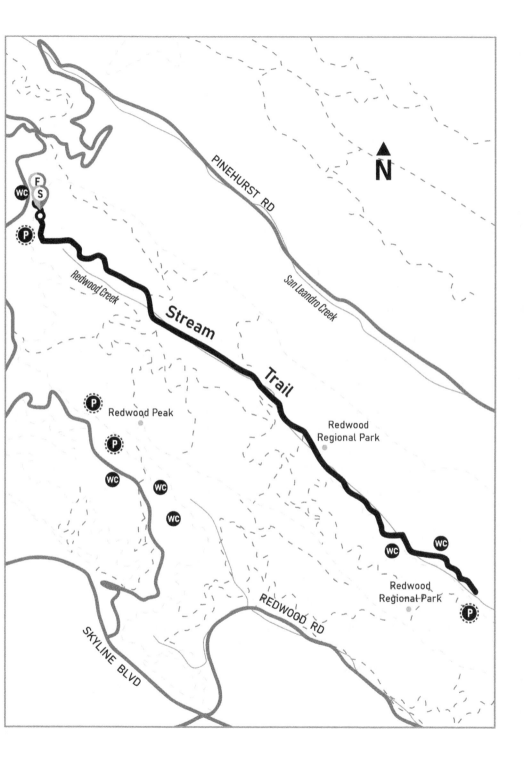

Cataract Falls, Tamalpais Watershed

The Cataract Falls trail runs through the Tamalpais Watershed, which is a drainage basin for Mt. Tamalpais. The trail is located in Marin County just over the Golden Gate Bridge from San Francisco.

It's a 4.8-mile trail that is best suited for older kids and teenagers, as the terrain can get rocky and steep. The trail ends at Cataract Falls and the lake in which the falls cascade. There are several waterfalls along the trail for kids and parents to see and take pictures. Dogs are allowed on the trail as long as they are on a leash. Bathrooms are not available.

Best time to visit: The trail is accessible all year round, but get there early, as it gets crowded as the day wears on.

Pass/permit/fees: It is free to enter Tamalpais Watershed.

How to get there: The watershed is located in Marin County north of San Francisco. The best way to access the park is by Highway 101 and exiting at the Mill Valley or Sir Francis Drake exits and allowing your GPS to guide you the rest of the way, as there many twists and turns to get to the gates of the park.

What to pack: Make sure to wear hiking boots and waterproof shoes as the terrain gets rocky, steep, and wet. It's a longer hike, so lots of snacks and water are great to have on hand and maybe some sandwiches for more nourishment.

What can you find? The park boasts vegetation like redwoods, oaks, firs, huckleberries, roses, and hazelnuts. Animals along the trail are woodpeckers, frogs, coyote, and deer.

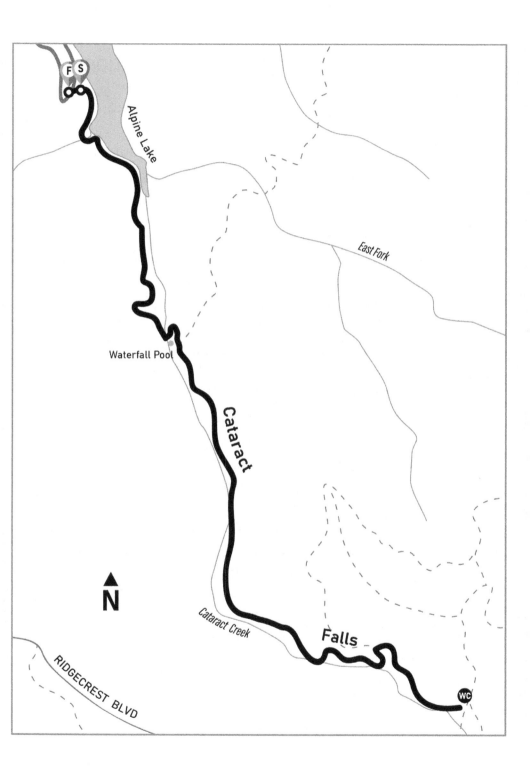

Hidden Falls Trail, Hidden Falls National Park

Hidden Falls National Park has about 30 miles of hiking trails in a vast oak woodland. You'll see hikers, bikers, and equestrian riders.

The Hidden Falls Trail is a 3.3-mile loop hike. It is great for older kids and teenagers, but some younger kids may also be able to handle the terrain. The trail ends at Hidden Falls. Dogs are allowed on the trail but must be on a leash. Bathrooms are available in the park. Cell phone service may be limited, so feel free to download the trail map before leaving on the hike.

Best time to visit: Hidden Falls Trail is best during the week, as the weekend gets very busy. The weekend gets so busy that it is recommended to make a reservation

Pass/permit/fees: On weekends and holidays it's $8. There are no fees or reservations Monday through Thursday.

How to get there: Hidden Falls is located in Auburn, California, just outside of Sacramento, on Highway 49. Highway 49 is easily accessible from Interstate 80.

What to pack: Pack long pants and long sleeves because the park has a lot of poison oak. Ankle support is necessary as this trail can get rocky and steep. Bring bug spray because in the grassier areas there are ticks. Snacks like trail mix and fruit are perfect for the hike, as is a lot of water.

What can you find? The park has flowers like California poppies, fuchsias, and lupines. Animals that are spotted along the trail are snakes (be careful!), squirrels, and deer.

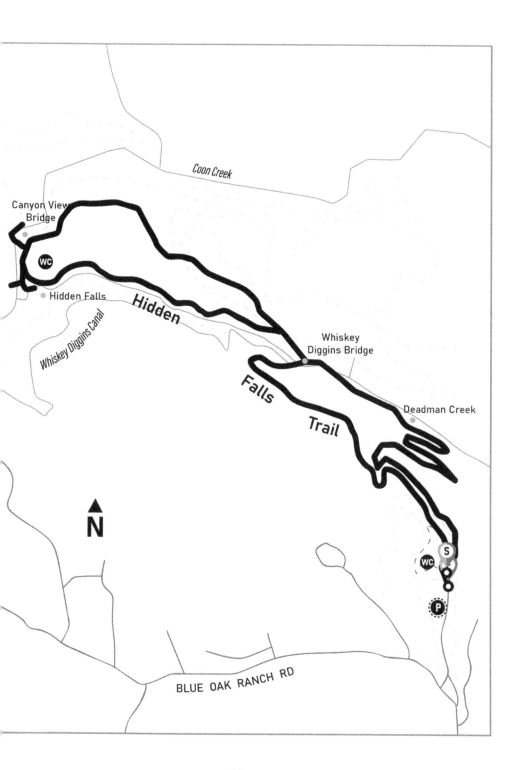

Valley View Trail, Big Sur

Big Sur is located near Monterey, California. It is one of the most popular state parks in California and offers culture, shopping, and outdoor activities.

The Valley View trail is a 1.8-mile loop through Big Sur that is great for toddlers and small children. The trail is not too difficult to walk, and there is a great view of the cove on the Pacific Ocean along the trail. Dogs are not allowed on this trail. Bathrooms are not available.

Best time to visit: Valley View Trail is accessible all year round. There is moderate traffic on the trail, so it's okay to go at any time of day.

Pass/permit/fees: It costs $10 to enter Pfeiffer Big Sur State Park.

How to get there: Pfeiffer Big Sur State Park is located off Highway 1 north of Carmel.

What to pack: Valley View Trail is a relatively short and easy trail to walk, so bring sunscreen and a hat for sunny days. Snacks like trail mix, fruit, or jerky are a good idea. Bring water.

What can you find? Valley View Trail is great for birdwatching, as there are 350 different types of birds, but you'll also see pumas, coyotes, foxes, and harbor seals. Sharks can be seen along the coast. You'll see redwoods, oaks, and grasslands.

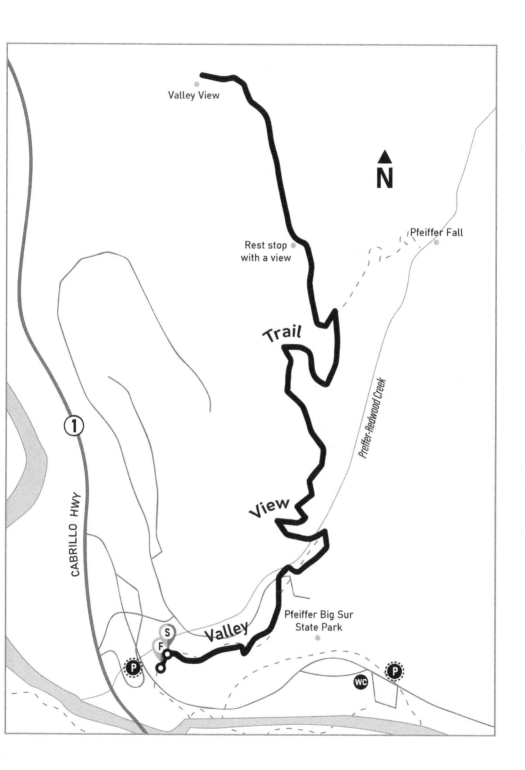

Soda Springs Trail, Big Sur

Soda Springs is a 5.8-mile trail that is best suited for older kids and teenagers. The trail is not extremely rocky or difficult, but it is a long trail and can get steep. The trail offers great views of Big Sur and the Pacific Ocean. Dogs are allowed on this trail, but they must be kept on a leash. There is not much parking available at the trailhead, so it's best to get there early.

Best time to visit: The Soda Springs Trail at Big Sur is accessible all year round. The trail does get some mild traffic and narrows in some spots, so the less people, the better.

Pass/permit/fees: It costs $10 to park at Los Padres National Forest Big Sur.

How to get there: The Soda Spring Trail is located on Highway 1 at mile marker MON 3.8.

What to pack: Sunblock and a hat. There is little-to-no shade on the Soda Springs trail. The trail is long, so bring snacks like trail mix, jerky, and fruit that won't spoil. Certain sandwiches are a great idea as well. Make sure your water bottle is full. Wear walking or hiking shoes with good support and soles, as you will be walking a long distance. Wear long pants and sleeves, as poison oak runs rampant in the area.

What can you find? There is a copious amount of California poppies along your hike. There is also a vast grassland as you approach the ocean. During the spring and fall, you can see whales migrating in the ocean.

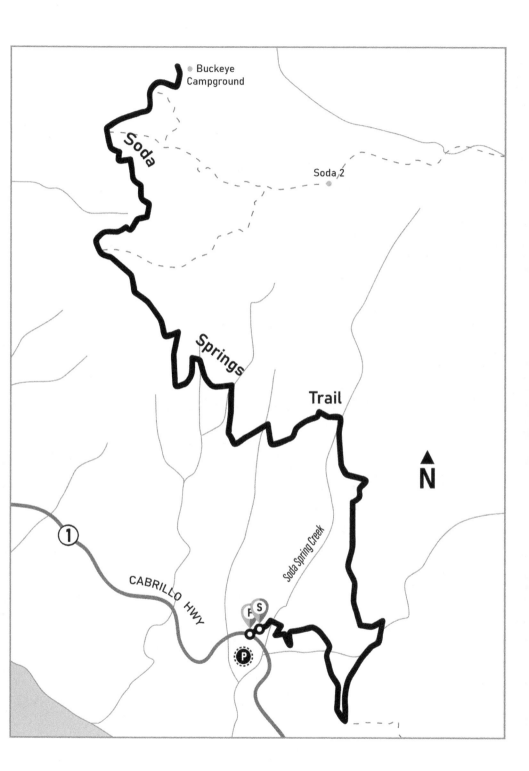

Buckeye Trail, Big Sur

The Buckeye Trail is a long, 8.6-mile trail that is best suited for teenagers. The trail can get difficult at times with inclines and rocky trail surfaces. The trail offers amazing views of the California coastline. Dogs are allowed on this trail, but there are a lot of ticks in this area so be cautious if you are bringing your dog on this hike.

Best time to visit: The trail is most beautiful in the fall but accessible June through November.

Pass/permit/fees: The trail is located by the side of the road, so free limited parking is available.

How to get there: The trailhead is off of Highway 1 at mile marker MON 2.4.

What to pack: The trail is long, so pack plenty of snacks and water. Jerky, trail mix, and fruit along with sandwiches that won't spoil are great options. Wear long pants and sleeves, as the area has an overabundance of ticks and poison oak. Wear good hiking boots with strong soles and ankle support, as the trail can get difficult.

What can you find? The hike starts with grasslands but gets dense with forest foliage of oaks, redwoods, laurels, and several wildflowers. Big Sur is home to coyotes, bobcats, seals, and foxes.

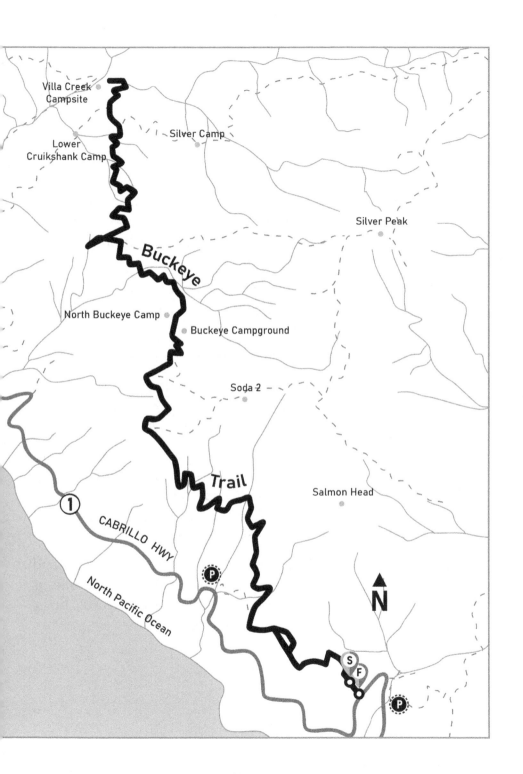

Vernal Falls, Yosemite National Park

Yosemite National Park is one of the most popular national parks in America known for its plethora of waterfalls.

The Vernal Falls trail is a 4-mile trail that is great for younger kids to teenagers. The trail ends at the gorgeous Vernal Falls. Dogs are not allowed on this trail, and bathrooms are not available near the trailhead. Certain parts of the trail are paved, making it a bit of an easier hike.

Best time to visit: Vernal Falls Trail is best taken between May and November. It is a popular trail and can get crowded, so going earlier in the day is better.

Pass/permit/fees: It costs $35 to enter Yosemite National Park.

How to get there: Yosemite National Park is located on Highway 140, which is accessible from Highway 120. Use your GPS from your location to access Highway 120.

What to pack: Due to the waterfall, the terrain of Vernal Falls trail can get slick and muddy, so make sure to wear hiking boots that have good traction for mud and wet ground. It's not too long of a hike, so light snacks and water are recommended. It gets sunny, so pack a hat and some sunblock.

What can you find? The trail is known for the sequoias and wildflowers that are present on the trail. The wildlife is extremely diverse and includes deer, frogs, trout, lizards, bugs, black bears, red foxes, and mountain lions.

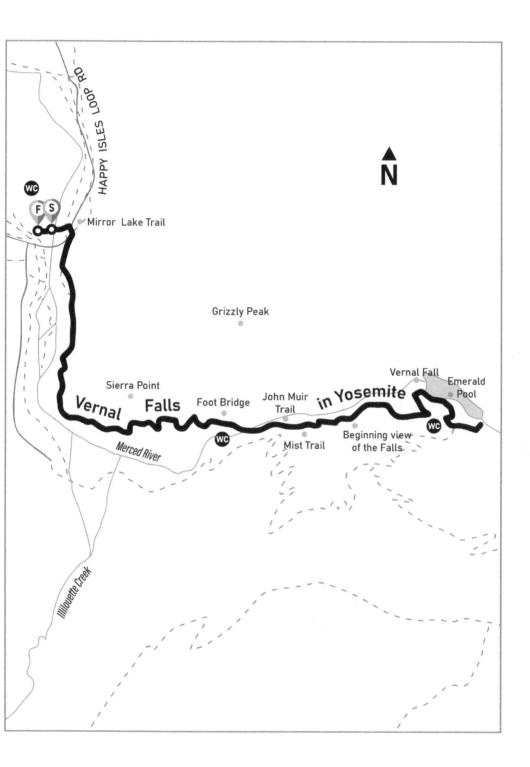

Lower Mariposa Grove, Yosemite National Park

Lower Mariposa Grove is a 6.2-mile hike that is best suited for older kids and teenagers due to the length of the hike, although some younger kids may be up for the adventure. Lower Mariposa Grove is home to famous trees like the Tunnel Tree and the Faithful Couple Tree.

The Tunnel Tree is the famous tree where the trunk has a tunnel cut through it so people can walk and drive along a trail. There is also a fallen tunnel tree that has created a new ecosystem in the park for animals, insects, and plant life. The Faithful Couple Tree is two trees that grew so close together their trunks fused together. Dogs are not allowed on this trail. Portable toilets are available by the trailhead.

Best time to visit: Lower Mariposa Grove Trail is accessible all year round. It is one of the most popular trails in all of California, so get there early before parking is limited.

Pass/permit/fees: It costs $35 to enter Yosemite National Park.

How to get there: Yosemite National Park is located on Highway 140, which is accessible from Highway 120. Use your GPS from your location to access Highway 120.

What to pack: Fill your water bottles before you head to the trail. There is a lot of walking, so sturdy hiking boots are a must. Fill your backpack with sandwiches that won't spoil, jerky, trail mix, and fruit for the long hike.

What can you find? Notice the giant sequoias, especially the Tunnel Tree, the Fallen Tunnel Tree, the Bachelor and Three Graces, the Grizzly Giant, and the Faithful Couple Tree. There are placards throughout the trail with the names of all the trees.

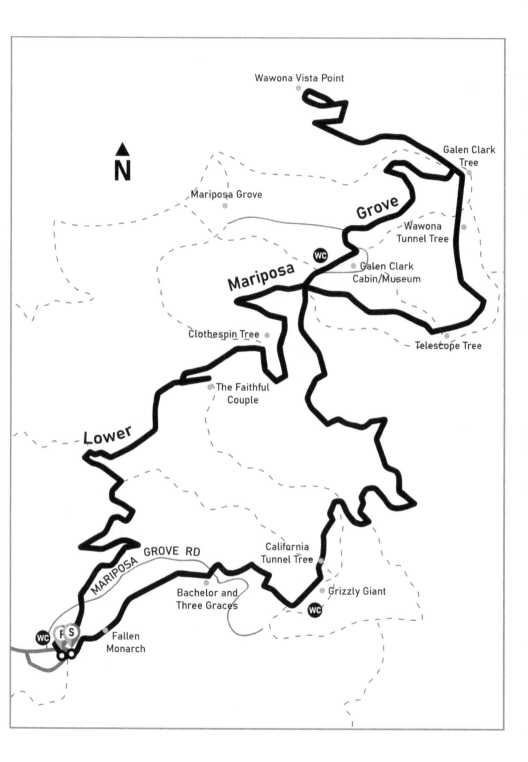

Grove Overlook Trail, Calaveras Big Trees State Park

Located in the Sierra Nevada mountain range, the Grove Overlook Trail winds through Calaveras Big Trees State Park. It is a 1.4-mile trail that is great for toddlers and younger kids, as the terrain remains relatively flat, and the hike is relatively short.

The Grove Overlook Trail is best known for going through two groves of sequoia trees. There are hundreds of sequoias along the way. Dogs are not allowed on this trail.

Best time to visit: The Grove Overlook Trail is accessible all year round. It is best to get there early.

Pass/permit/fees: It costs $4 to enter Calaveras Big Trees State Park.

How to get there: Calaveras Big Trees State Park is located on Highway 4, which is accessed from Highway 99. Use your GPS to get you to Highway 99.

What to pack: Bring plenty of water and snacks for the trail. Wear sturdy hiking shoes in the event that the terrain gets a bit bumpy or rough. Always bring sunblock and a hat for sunny days.

What can you find? There are dozens of different tree species including dogwood, sugar pine, white fir, incense cedar, and ponderosa pines. Flowers you will see are leopard lily, monkeyflower, hyacinth, and lupines. Be on the lookout for bears, squirrels, and a large variety of different bird species.

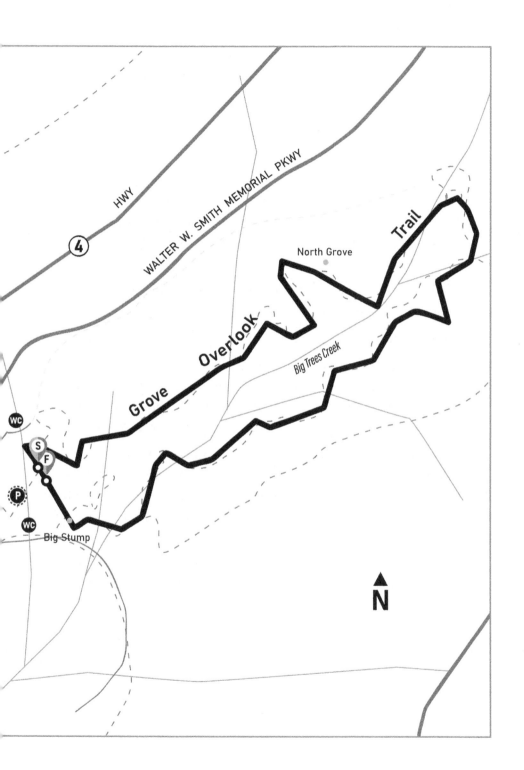

Sequoia Nature Trail, Portola State Park

The Sequoia Nature Trail is a 1.5-mile hike that is great for toddlers and younger kids. Older kids and teenagers will also enjoy this hike.

Portola State Park is 2,800 acres of redwood trees. The park is known for its myriad of creeks that run through the park, waterfalls, and the mighty redwoods. Dogs are not allowed on this trail, and bathrooms are located in the visitor center.

Best time to visit: The Sequoia Nature Trail is accessible all year round. The trail gets moderately busy.

Pass/permit/fees: It costs $10 to enter Portola State Park.

How to get there: Portola State Park is located on Portola State Park Road, which is accessible from Highway 35 via Alpine Road. There is limited-to-no cell phone reception, so make sure to print out any maps or direction before starting your trip.

What to pack: Snacks like trail mix and fruit are a good choice. There are many creeks to cross and sometimes there aren't bridges, so waterproof hiking shoes or water shoes with sturdy soles are a must to keep dry. Bring sunblock and a hat for the sunnier days.

What can you find? Aside from the redwoods and sequoias that are indigenous to the area, you will also see ferns and huckleberries. The wildlife showcases black-tailed deer and mountain lions, along with banana slugs, rainbow trout, and coho salmon.

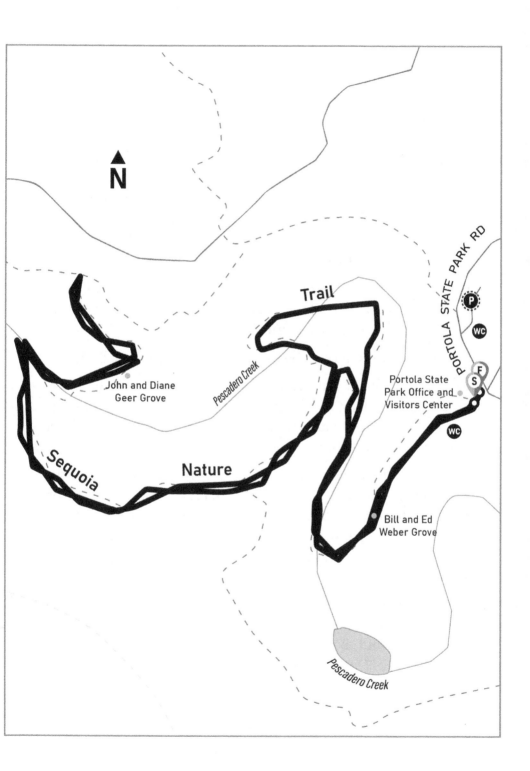

Chickadee Trail, Huddart County Park

Huddart County Park is located just south of San Francisco in San Mateo County. Huddart is 900 acres of hiking trails, wildlife, and redwoods.

The Chickadee Trail is less than 1 mile long and is perfect for toddlers and younger kids. Dogs are not allowed on this trail. Bathrooms are located in picnic areas near the trail. This trail is wheelchair accessible.

Best time to visit: The trail is accessible all year round. Due to its short length, the trail never gets too busy, so it's a good trail to go on if your little one wants to move slow.

Pass/permit/fees: It costs $6 to enter Huddart County Park.

How to get there: Huddart County Park is located on Kings Mountain Road in Woodside, California, which is accessible from Highway 280 via Woodside Road. Consult your GPS for more detailed directions.

What to pack: Make sure to have light snacks on hand for the short hike, as well as water. Sunblock and a hat are perfect on a sunny day. Wear long pants, as the trail has poison oak on it, and wear your hiking boots or sneakers because of rattlesnakes. No sandals or open toed shoes will help you stay safe.

What can you find? Keep an eye out for black-tailed deer, gray squirrels, bobcats, brush rabbits, opossums, lizards, and of course, chestnut backed chickadees. Among the redwoods, you will see Douglas firs, golden back fern, and several different kinds of fungi.

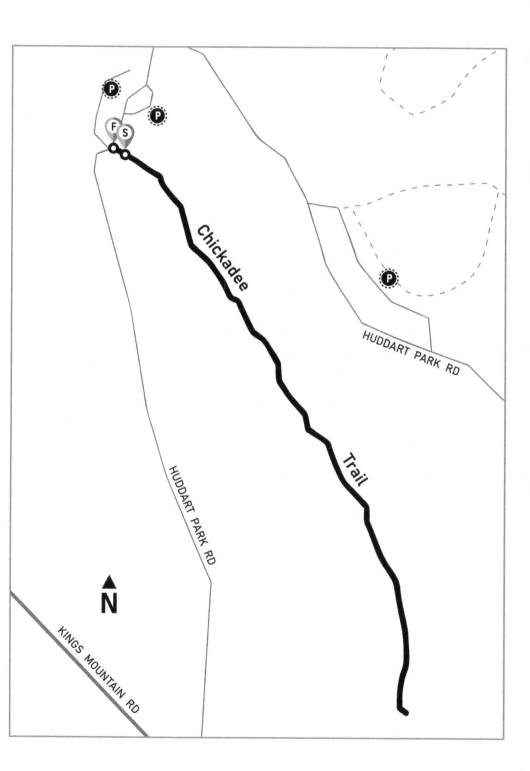

Edison Point Trail, Sierra National Forest

Sierra National Forest is best known for its lakes. The forest is located between King Canyon Park and Yosemite National Park.

The Edison Point Trail is about 2 miles long and is best suited for younger kids to teenagers. Toddlers may have some difficulty with the trail. Dogs are allowed on this trail but must be kept on a leash. Bathrooms are located near picnic areas and the welcome center.

Best time to visit: The Edison Point Trail is accessible all year round. The trail can get moderately busy.

Pass/permit/fees: It costs $6 per permit and $5 per person to enter Sierra National Forest.

How to get there: Sierra National Forest is accessible from Highway 140 via Highway 99. Check your GPS for more detailed directions.

What to pack: Definitely bring bug spray. There are lots of ticks on the trail. Wear long pants and hiking boots above the ankle for added security against ticks. Pack sunblock, as the trail is mostly walked through a grassland with very little covering. A hat is also a good idea. Bring plenty of water and some snacks for this relatively short hike.

What can you find? There is a beautiful view of one of the park's many lakes during your hike. Black-tailed deer are spotted here and there, and grasslands offer wildflowers of yellow, red, and violet.

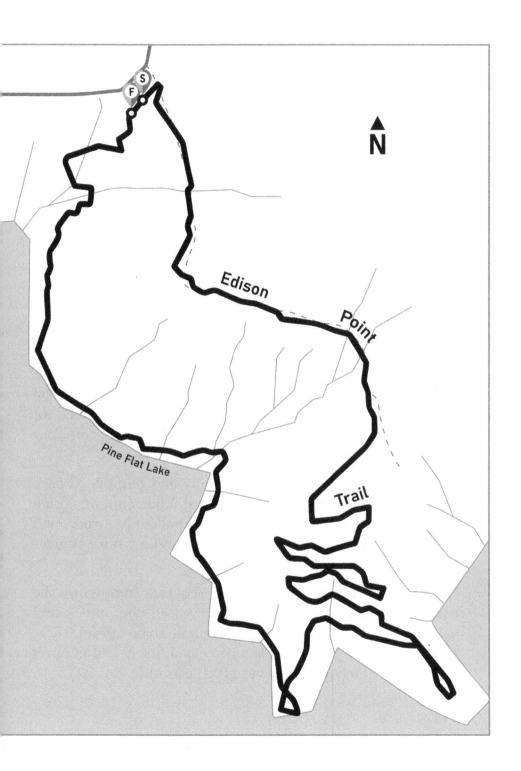

The Giant Forest Trail, Sequoia National Park

Sequoia National Park is home to about 8,000 sequoia trees.

The Giant Forest Trail is a long 7-mile hike that is best suited for teenagers. Parking is quite limited, so it may be better to park at the visitor center and take a shuttle to the trailhead. Dogs are not allowed on this trail. Bathrooms are not located near the trail.

Best time to visit: The Giant Forest Trail is best between May and October. Get there early to avoid the crowds.

Pass/permit/fees: It is $35 to enter Sequoia National Park. The fee can be paid online ahead of time.

How to get there: Sequoia National Park is located on California Highway 180 via Highway 99. Check your GPS for more detailed directions to Highway 99 depending on your starting point.

What to pack: The terrain can get hilly and bumpy, so pack hiking shoes that are sturdy with great ankle support. Bring plenty of water. Bring snacks like trail mix, fruit, and sandwiches. Bring sunblock, sunglasses, and a hat for sunnier and warmer days.

What can you find? Aside from the sequoias from which the park gets its name, you will see buckwheat, lilies, pines, and oaks. There are bears along the hiking trail, so be careful. There are also foxes, bobcats, and skunks. Quail, mice, and gophers run around. Some trees are over 2,000 years old.

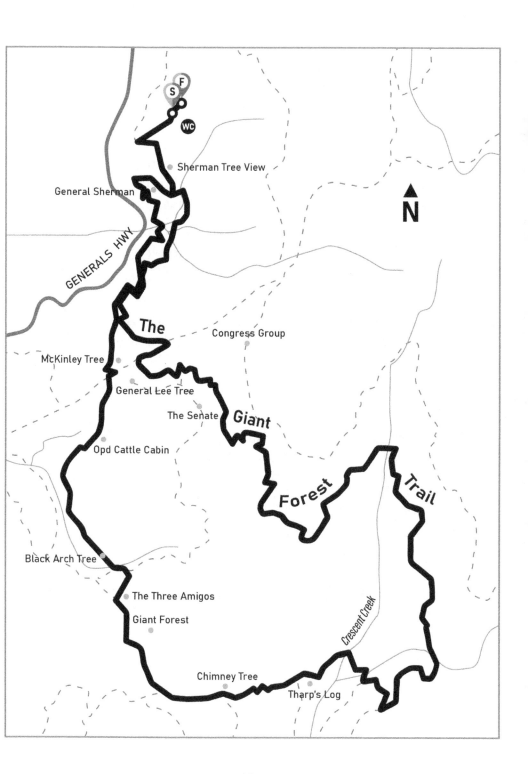

Dana Point Headlands, Dana Point Headlands Nature Preserve

The Dana Point Headlands Trail is a 1-mile trail that is great for toddlers and younger children. The visitor center has a lot of information on the geological history of the preserve.

The nature preserve is home to hundreds of species of plants whose habitats are protected to ensure the prolonged life of all the species. Dogs are not allowed on this trail, and bathrooms are located at the visitor center.

Best time to visit: The Dana Point Trail is accessible all year round. The trail is both paved and dirt path. There are amazing views of Dana Point Harbor.

Pass/permit/fees: It costs $15 to enter Dana Point Headlands Nature Preserve.

How to get there: California State Highway 1 begins in Dana Point. Highway 1 can be accessed via Interstate 5.

What to pack: Bring plenty of sunblock and a hat. The hike is short, so light snacks and plenty of water are recommended.

What can you find? The Ocean Institute Museum is located at Dana Point. Check their website for their latest indoor and outdoor activities for the whole family. While there, you can learn all about the wildlife of the nature preserve.

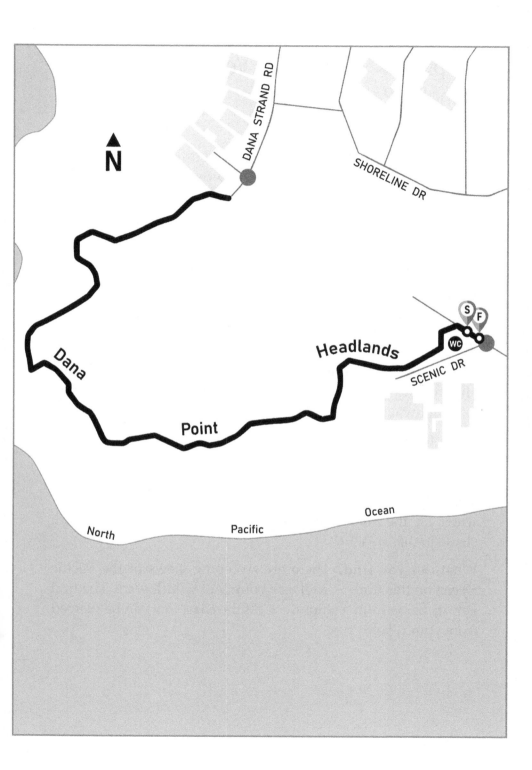

Shipwreck Trail, Palos Verdes Peninsula, Rancho Palos Verdes

Rancho Palos Verdes is a sub region of Los Angeles that offers a number of hiking trails. The Shipwreck Trail is a 4.6-mile hike that is best suited for older kids to teenagers.

Dogs are allowed on the trails but must be kept on a leash. Bathrooms are available in the park.

Best time to visit: The Shipwreck Trail is accessible all year round.

Pass/permit/fees: Parking and entrance to the peninsula are free.

How to get there: Rancho Palos Verdes is located off of State Highway 1. Check your GPS for specific directions once you exit Highway 1.

What to pack: In this coastal location, a light jacket may be required during certain times of the year. The trails can get very rocky and uneven, so wear good hiking shoes with ankle support and sturdy soles. Pack some snacks and plenty of water for the hike. Sunblock is a must, as there is not much shade in this area.

What can you find? There are sweeping views of the Pacific Ocean on this trail, as well as a bounty of wildflowers. The trail gets its name from a shipwreck off the coast that can be viewed from your hike.

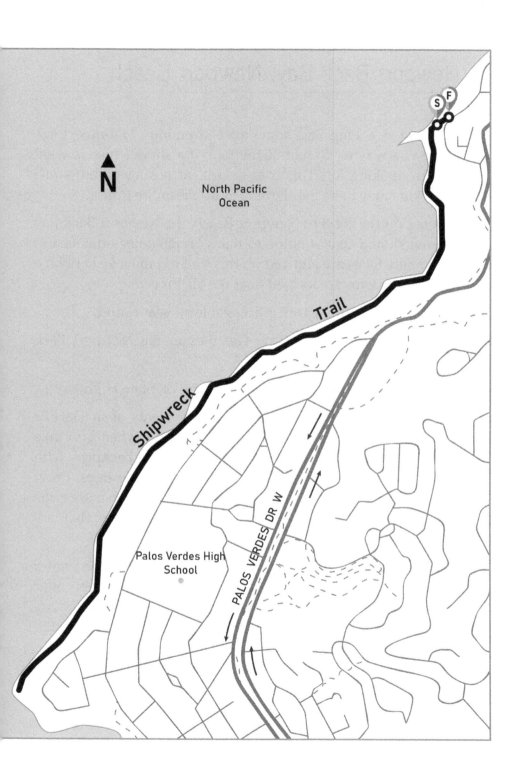

Newport Back Bay, Newport Beach

The trail is a long and sometimes strenuous 11.4-mile loop. There is a way to do half of the loop if a shorter hike is what you are looking for. This trail is best for teenagers, but some older kids may have the stamina to do the entire trail.

Located off the coast of Newport Beach, the Newport Back Bay is a marshland that is home to many indigenous animals and vegetation. Dogs are allowed on this trail but must be kept on a leash. Bathrooms are located near the visitor center.

Best time to visit: The trail is accessible all year round.

Pass/permit/fees: There is no fee to enter the Newport Back Bay.

How to get there: The Back Bay is located on State Highway 1.

What to pack: This is a long trail, so pack plenty of snacks like trail mix and fruit plus some sandwiches for when you take breaks. Pack plenty of water and maybe even a backpack with a bladder. This area is an estuary, so there are no trees. Bring sunblock, sunglasses, and a hat. Because of the marsh area, the trail can get muddy, so wear good hiking boots that are waterproof.

What can you find? The Newport Back Bay Aquatic Center and Science Center are in the park. These centers offer information on the history and wildlife of the park. There are also a few other nature stops along the trail like the dunes, Big Canyon, and Vista Point.

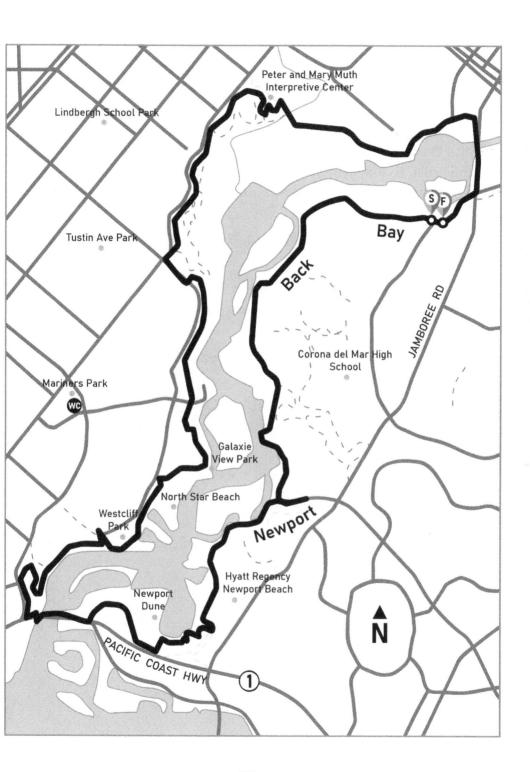

Laurel Canyon Trail, Laguna Beach

Laguna Coastal Wilderness Park is home to several canyons and the only natural lakes of Orange County. The trail is a 3.3-mile hike that is best suited for younger kids up to teenagers. The trail is mixed with the Laurel Spur Trail and the Willow Trail.

Dogs are not allowed on this trail. Bathrooms are located in the Nature Center.

Best time to visit: Laurel Canyon Trail is accessible all year round; however, the trail gets very crowded, so it is best to visit on the weekends.

Pass/permit/fees: It costs $3 to park at Laguna Coast Wilderness Park.

How to get there: Laguna Coast Wilderness Park is located on Highway 133, which is accessible from either Interstate 405 or Highway 1.

What to pack: The trail can get rocky, so bring sturdy hiking boots. Sunblock and a hat are a must, as well as snacks for the trail like fruit, trail mix, or protein bars.

What can you find? Besides the number of canyons in the area, there are also lakes and waterfalls.

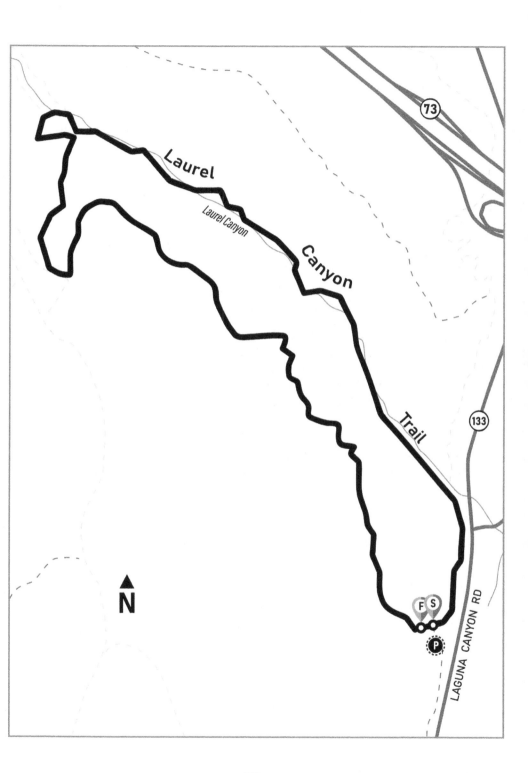

Top of the World, Laguna Beach

Top of the World is a 2.4-mile hike that is best suited for younger kids to teenagers. The trail gets very steep in some places, so toddlers may not be suited for the terrain.

Dogs are allowed on the trail but must be kept on a leash. Bathrooms are located at the Nature Center.

Best time to visit: The trail is accessible all year round. The trail usually doesn't get too busy, so any time of day is a good time to go. The trail does close after periods of rain due to the steep inclines, so check the weather before you plan your trip.

Pass/permit/fees: It costs $3 to park at Laguna Coast Wilderness Park.

How to get there: Laguna Coast Wilderness Park is located on Highway 133, which is accessible from either Interstate 405 or Highway 1.

What to pack: The trail can get rocky, so bring sturdy hiking boots. Sunblock and a hat are a must, as well as snacks for the trail like fruit, trail mix, or protein bars.

What can you find? Top of the World gives you gorgeous views of Southern California and neighboring areas.

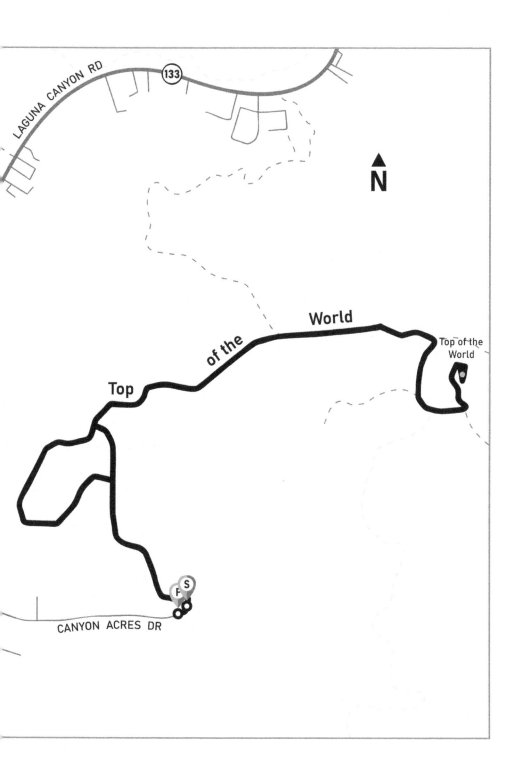

Santa Ynez Falls Trail, Topanga State Park

Part of the Santa Monica mountain range, Topanga State Park is located in Los Angeles. It is the largest wildland within the limits of a major American city.

Santa Ynez is a 2.3-mile trail that is good for younger kids to teenagers. Dogs are not allowed in Topanga State Park. Bathrooms are located at the welcome center.

Best time to visit: Santa Ynez Falls is accessible all year round.

Pass/permit/fees: It costs $10 to park at Topanga State Park; however, there is free parking on the road outside of the park.

How to get there: Topanga State park is located on Entrada Road, which is accessible from State Highway 101.

What to pack: Make sure to wear good hiking shoes, as the terrain can get uneven and rocky, and the waterfall can make some of the path slippery. Hiking boots above the ankle are recommended, as are long pants since the park has a large amount of poison oak. Since it is grasslands, there is not much shade, so wear sunblock and bring a hat. Pack light snacks like protein bars and jerky, and always have plenty of water.

What can you find? The geological area of Topanga State Park was formed by volcanoes and earthquakes, so there is a large number of geological formations to see. Black bears have been known to come close to the trail, so as with all wildlife, be careful.

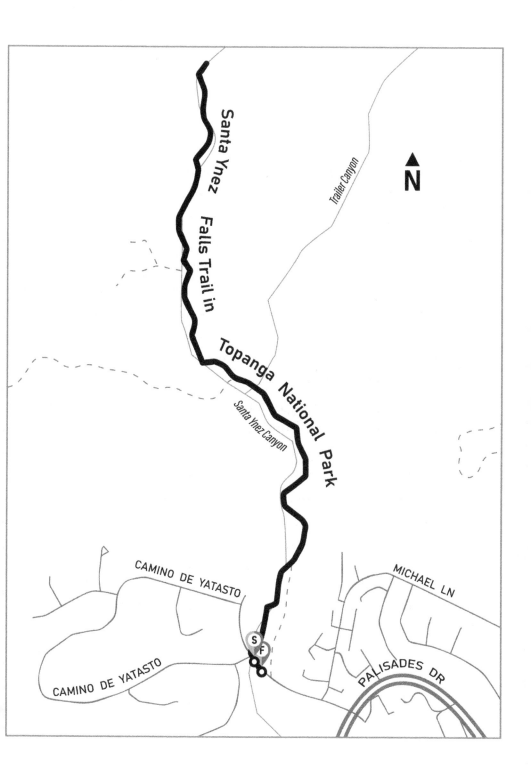

Murphy Ranch Trail, Topanga State Park

Murphy Ranch Trail is a 3.4-mile hike that is best suited for younger kids to teenagers. To make hiking up the terrain easier, there are several sets of stairs throughout the trail — 542, to be exact. Some of the stairs do not have railings, so leave the toddlers off this trail.

Dogs are allowed on the trail but must be kept on a leash. Bathrooms are located at the visitor center.

Best time to visit: The Murphy Ranch Trail gets very crowded, so the best time to go is midday. The trail is accessible all year round.

Pass/permit/fees: To park in Topanga State Park there is a $10 fee, but parking is free on the road outside of the park.

How to get there: Topanga State Park is located on Entrada Road, which is accessible from State Highway 101.

What to pack: Wear sturdy hiking boots and bring snacks and water for the hike. Wear sunblock and take a hat. Pack lightly, as there are stairs to climb.

What can you find? There are plenty of snakes in the area, so be careful. Once you get along the trail, there are beautiful views of Topanga State Park and Pacific Palisades. The area is mostly grassland, and you will see a large number of wildflowers. There are also the remains of buildings used during World War II.

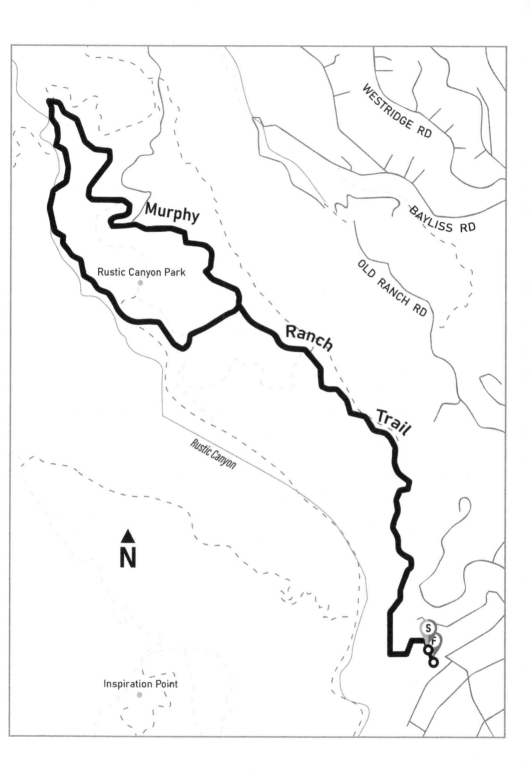

Discovery Trail, Franklin Canyon Park

Franklin Canyon Park is located between the San Fernando Valley and Beverly Hills. It was once a reservoir for the area that has since been turned into a park. It is home to 605 acres of land for animals and trees.

The hike is a very short .6-mile trek that is perfect for a day trip with toddlers or younger kids. Dogs are allowed on a leash, and bathrooms are available at the park entrance.

Best time to visit: The Discovery Trail is accessible all year round.

Pass/permit/fees: It is free to park at Franklin Canyon.

How to get there: Franklin Canyon is in Beverly Hills, California. Set your GPS for exact directions.

What to pack: The trail is short, and the park is small; pack light snacks and water for the hike. Any other food can be found within Beverly Hills and the surrounding area. Always wear sunblock and a hat to protect against the sun.

What can you find? Franklin Canyon has lakes that you can hike around. There are also many wildflowers and walnut trees, oaks, and grasslands. There is a plaque in the park that denotes the exact geographical center of Los Angeles.

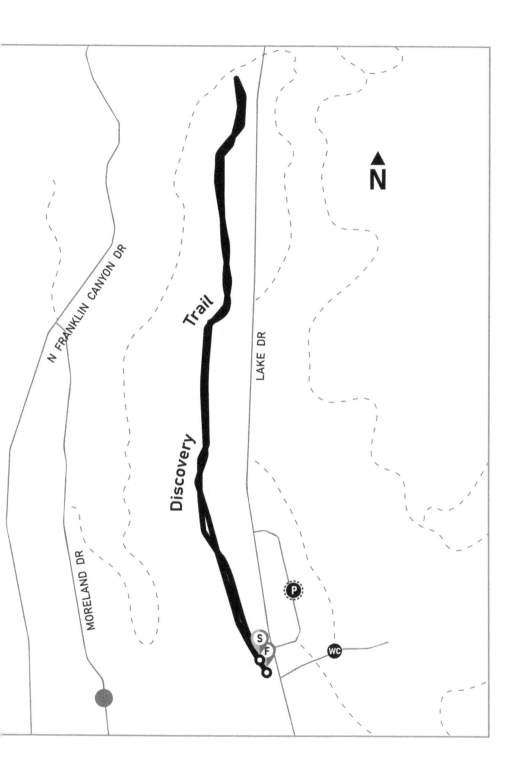

Oso Creek Trail, Mission Viejo

Oso Creek Trail is a 3.2-mile hike that is good for toddlers to older kids. The terrain is relatively flat and easy to hike.

Mission Viejo sits on a land grant that was issued by the Spanish. It is considered the greatest master-planned community ever built. All the roads and layouts of the city are in direct correlation to the natural topography of the region. Dogs are allowed on this trail but must be kept on a leash, and bathrooms are not located on the trail but in a neighboring park. Strollers have access to this trail, as do wheelchairs.

Best time to visit: The trail is best used from March to October. It is also best to go early in the day, as the trail gets a lot of traffic.

Pass/permit/fees: Parking is free in Mission Viejo on the streets of the city and in the park.

How to get there: Mission Viejo is located on Interstate Highway 5. Use your GPS for more detailed directions on how to reach the trail head once you exit the interstate.

What to pack: Bring sunblock, a hat, and plenty of water for your hike. Light snacks are good to bring to eat while you are hiking.

What can you find? Oso Creek Trail winds along a creek, so there are plenty of beautiful views. There is a butterfly garden on the trail and a hedge maze for little kids to play in. There is also a plant garden. Kids may see rabbits, lizards, and lots of birds.

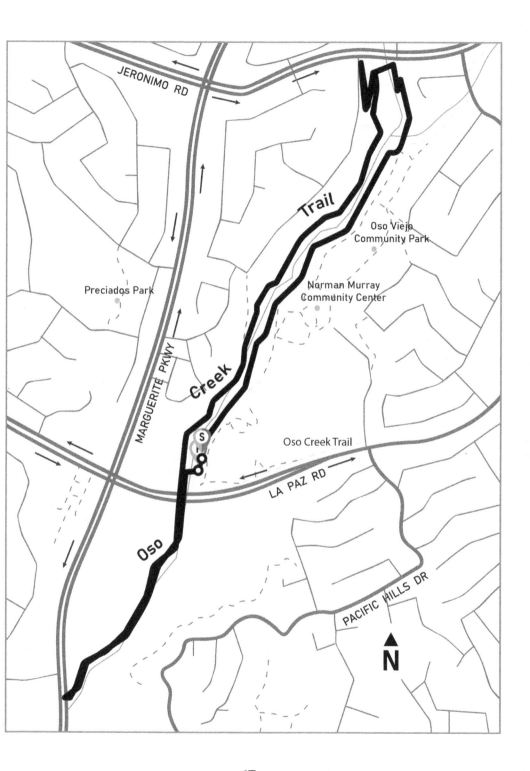

Wilderness Glen Park, Mission Viejo

Wilderness Glen is a 4-mile trail that is great for younger kids to teenagers. The trail is relatively flat, and both paved and unpaved. Located in Mission Viejo, it is an urban hike with a lot to see.

Dogs are allowed on the trail but must be kept on a leash. Bathrooms are located in the neighboring park.

Best time to visit: Wilderness Glen is accessible all year round but best from spring to fall. The park can get crowded, so try and go early.

Pass/permit/fees: It is free to park on the streets of Mission Viejo.

How to get there: Mission Viejo is located on Interstate Highway 5. Use your GPS for more detailed directions on how to reach the trail head once you exit the Interstate.

What to pack: Bring sunblock, a hat, and plenty of water for your hike. Light snacks are good to bring to eat while you are hiking.

What can you find? There are lots of rabbits and hawks along the trail as well as wildflowers and plants along the creek.

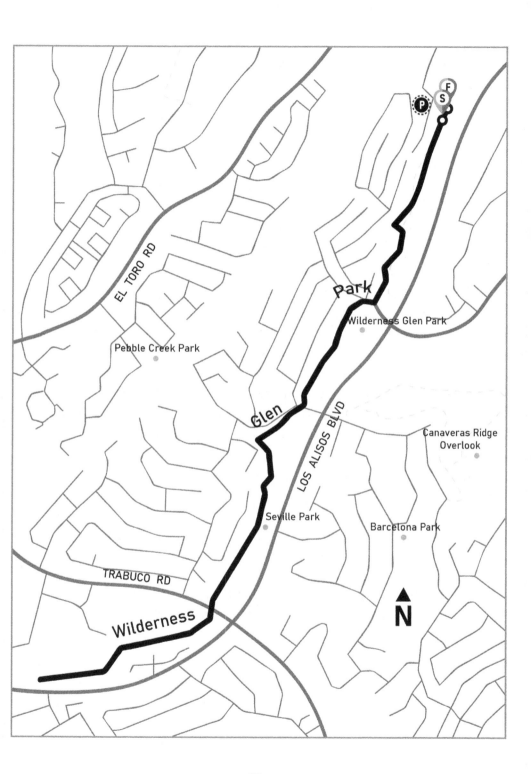

Pictograph Trail, Anza-Borrego Desert State Park

This state park gets its name from two sources: Juan Bautista de Anza, who was a Spanish explorer, and the Spanish word for sheep: borrego.

This trail is a 2.6-mile trail that is best suited for younger kids to teenagers. Dogs are not allowed on this trail. Bathrooms are located at the visitor center and at camp sites.

Best time to visit: The Pictograph Trail is best during the months of May through October.

Pass/permit/fees: It costs $10 to enter Anza-Borrego Desert State park.

How to get there: Anza-Borrego Desert State Park is located in Borrego Springs, CA, on Highway 22. Use your GPS for detailed directions to easily access Highway 22 from your location.

What to pack: Sunblock, hat, sunglasses, and light clothing are musts. Bring plenty of water for your hike. The terrain is sandy and rocky, so wear hiking boots with sturdy soles and ankle support. Bring snacks that won't spoil in the heat like trail mix, protein bars, and dried fruit.

What can you find? On the pictograph trail, you will find pictographs decorating a lot of the desert rocks. There is also a dry waterfall where the trail ends.

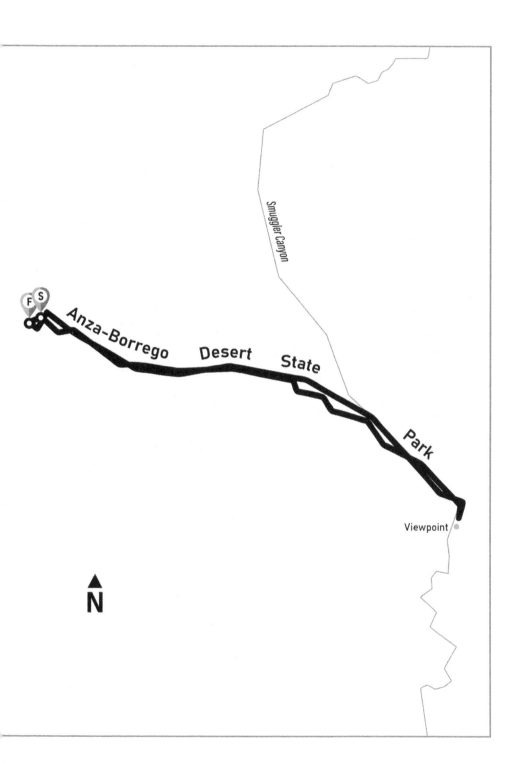

Smuggler Canyon

F S

Anza-Borrego Desert State Park

Viewpoint

N

Cactus Loop Trail, Anza-Borrego Desert State Park

The Cactus Loop Trail is a short .7-mile trail that is great for toddlers and younger kids. This trail is a great way to introduce your young ones to desert hiking. It's a quick loop that will allow the youngest hikers to experience the desert without the harshness of a full-on hike. Dogs are not allowed on the trial, and bathrooms are located at camp sites and the visitor center.

Best time to visit: The Cactus Loop Trail is best from October through May when it's not too hot for young kids. The trail does get moderate traffic but going early ensures it won't be too crowded and the temperature won't be too hot.

Pass/permit/fees: It costs $10 to enter Anza-Borrego Desert State Park.

How to get there: Anza-Borrego Desert State Park is located in Borrego Springs, CA, on Highway 22. Use your GPS to find the best way to access Highway 22 from your location.

What to pack: Even though the hike is short, bring plenty of sunblock, a hat, sunglasses, light clothing, and plenty of water. Light snacks like trail mix and dried fruit are optimal. The terrain is sandy and rocky, so sturdy hiking shoes are a must with great ankle support. High socks will keep sand and dirt out of your boots and off your legs.

What can you find? Be on the lookout for blooming cacti throughout the trail with lots of wildflowers on the trek. You may spot a bobcat, mountain lion, rabbits, or big horn sheep.

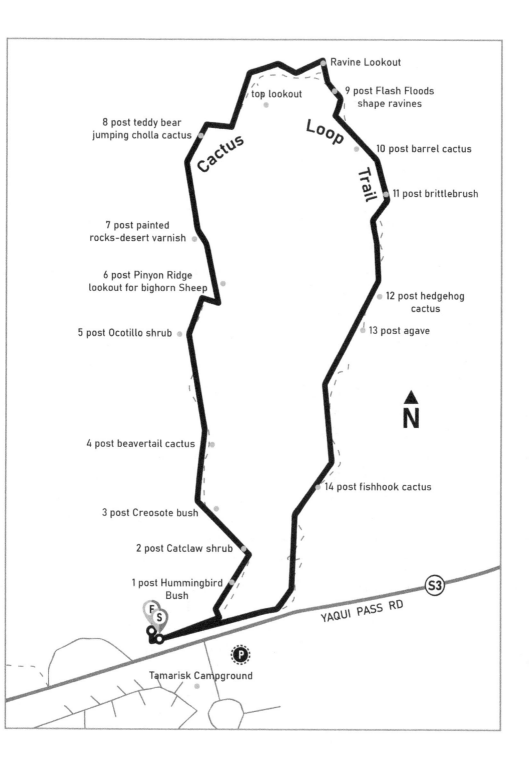

Ravine Lookout

9 post Flash Floods
shape ravines

top lookout

8 post teddy bear
jumping cholla cactus

Cactus

Loop

10 post barrel cactus

Trail

11 post brittlebrush

7 post painted
rocks-desert varnish

6 post Pinyon Ridge
lookout for bighorn Sheep

12 post hedgehog
cactus

5 post Ocotillo shrub

13 post agave

N

4 post beavertail cactus

14 post fishhook cactus

3 post Creosote bush

2 post Catclaw shrub

1 post Hummingbird
Bush

F
S

S3

YAQUI PASS RD

P

Tamarisk Campground

Elephant Trees Nature Trail, Anza-Borrego Desert State Park

Elephant Trees Nature Trail is a 2.1-mile hike that is best suited for younger kids to teenagers. The terrain is fairly flat, so there won't be too much exertion on this hike.

Dogs are not allowed on the trail, and bathrooms are located at the visitor center and at camp sites.

Best time to visit: Elephant Trees Nature Trail is accessible all year round but may be best in the winter months when the temperature is not too hot.

Pass/permit/fees: It costs $10 to enter Anza-Borrego Desert State Park.

How to get there: Anza-Borrego Desert State Park is located on Highway 22 in Borrego Springs, CA. Use your GPS to find the best way to access Highway 22 from your location.

What to pack: Make sure to bring plenty of water in multiple bottles or in a bladder in your backpack. Wear sunblock, a hat, and sunglasses. The terrain is rocky and sandy, so hiking boots with great ankle support are a must. High socks will help keep sand and dust out of your shoes and off your legs. Bring trail mix, dried fruit, or protein bars, as they won't spoil in the heat.

What can you find? There are 13 nature spots along the trail where you can see cacti, wildflowers, and some of the wildlife of the park like bobcats, lions, and rabbits. Visit the Anza-Borrego Desert State Park visitors center for a detailed map of the trail and where to stop as you hike.

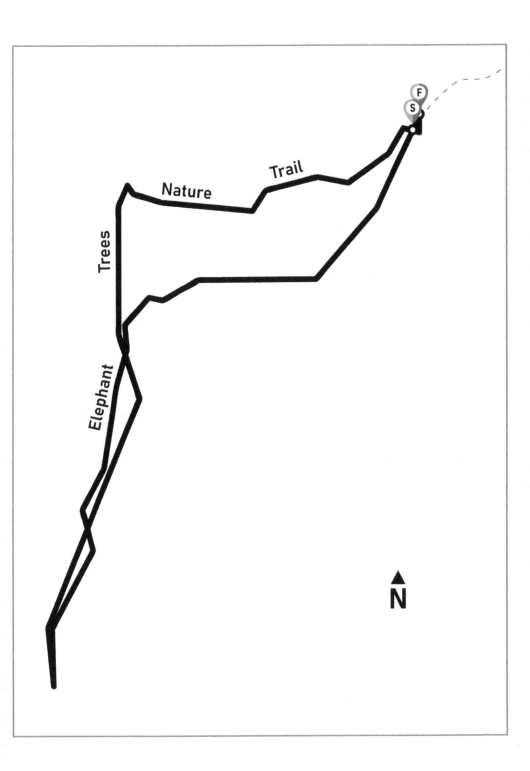

Yaqui Well Nature Trail, Anza-Borrego State Park

Yaqui Well Nature Trail is a 1.7-mile hike that is best suited for toddlers and younger kids. It's a great, quick hike to take if you are spending the day in the park or simply passing through.

Dogs are not allowed on the trail, and bathrooms are located in the visitor center and campsites.

Best time to visit: The trail is best used October through April when the temperatures are not too hot.

Pass/permit/fees: It costs $10 to enter Anza-Borrego Desert State Park.

How to get there: Anza-Borrego Desert State Park is located on Highway 22 in Borrego Springs, CA. Use your GPS to find the best way to access Highway 22 from your location. The trail itself is located off of Highway 78.

What to pack: Bring sunblock, a hat, and sunglasses for the desert weather. Pack plenty of water due to the dry climate. Small snacks like a protein bar or trail mix are great for this short hike.

What can you find? Yaqui Well is named for an old watering hole in the area. Most of the well is dried, but it can still be viewed. The trail is also known for blooming cacti and bird watching.

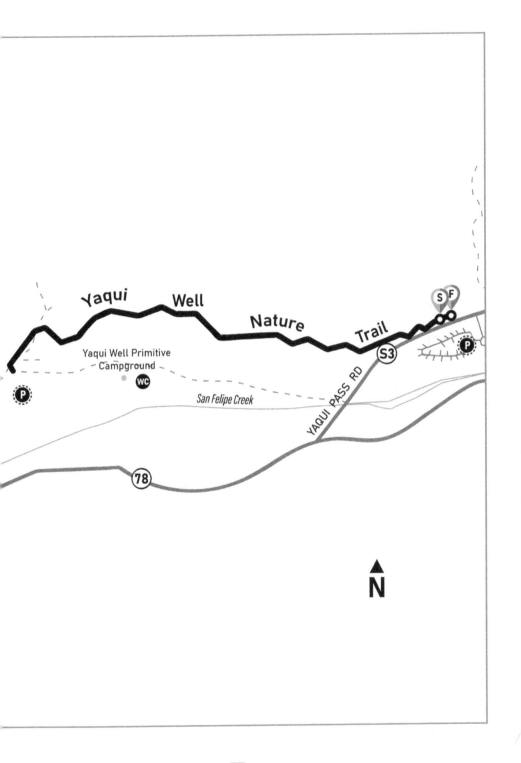

Yaqui Well Nature Trail

Yaqui Well Primitive Campground

San Felipe Creek

YAQUI PASS RD

S3

78

N

Barker Dam Nature Trail, Joshua Tree

Joshua Tree State Park is named after the Joshua Tree that is popular throughout the area. The park sits between the Mojave Desert and the Colorado Desert. There are views of Coachella Valley and Hidden Valley.

The Barker Dam Nature Trail is a 1.3-mile hike that is great for toddlers and younger kids. It's a relatively flat trail that is easy to hike with a lot of trees. At times, you may see animals hanging out around the dam for water. Dogs are not allowed on this trail. Phone service is not great, so GPS cannot be used within the park. Bathrooms are located in the visitor centers.

Best time to visit: The views are best experienced at sunset. The trail is accessible all year round.

Pass/permit/fees: It costs $25 to park at Joshua Tree State Park.

How to get there: Joshua Tree is accessible from either Interstate 10 or Highway 62.

What to pack: For this desert hike, bring plenty of water, sunblock, sunglasses, a hat, and light snacks like trail mix and jerky.

What can you find? Joshua Tree has two distinct ecosystems of desert and heavy rains. After rain, animals come out for the water, so you may see bobcats and birds. The area is famous for the twisting and turning spikey Joshua Tree that looks like something out of a fantasy novel.

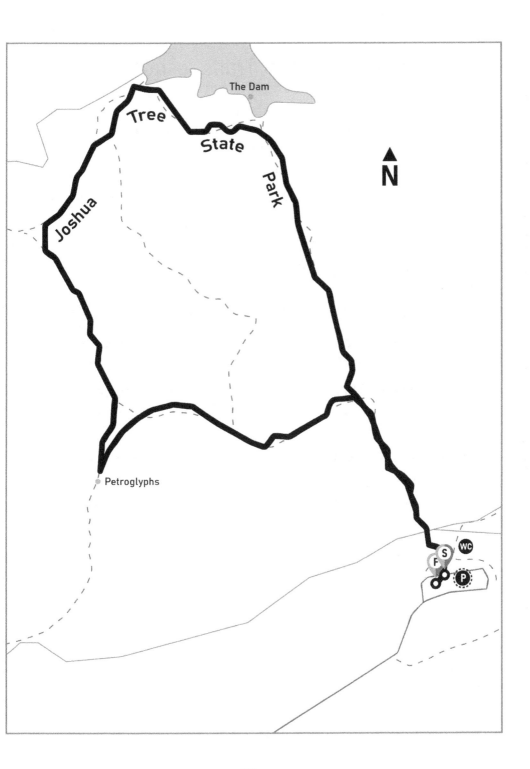

Mastodon Peak Loop Trail, Joshua Tree

Mastodon Peak Loop Trail is a 2.6-mile trail that is great for younger kids to teenagers. The hike is relatively easy, so it's a nice trip that is not too strenuous.

Dogs are not allowed on this trail. Bathrooms are located in the visitor centers. GPS will not work in the park, so download a map before heading out.

Best time to visit: The trail is best used from April through October.

Pass/permit/fees: It costs $25 to park at Joshua Tree State Park.

How to get there: Joshua Tree is accessible from either Interstate 10 or Highway 62.

What to pack: There is little-to-no shade, so bring plenty of sunblock, sunglasses, a hat, water, and snacks like jerky and trail mix.

What can you find? The trail offers some climbing for older kids if they want to access Mastodon Peak. There is an old mine on the trail that can be viewed from the trail as well as a beautiful view of the Salton Sea. Lots of desert flowers and blooming cacti can be seen.

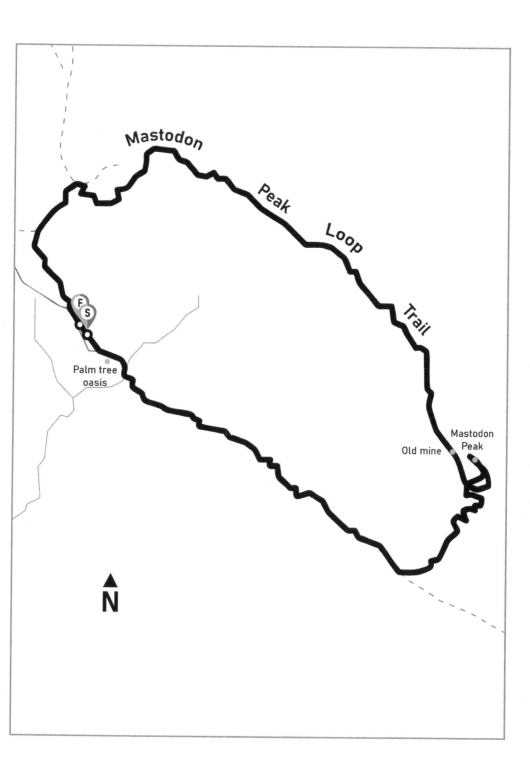

Mastodon

Peak

Loop

Trail

F
S

Palm tree
oasis

Old mine

Mastodon
Peak

N

Wall Street Mill Trail, Joshua Tree

Wall Street Mill Trail is a 2.4-mile trail that is great for younger kids to teenagers. It is a relatively flat trail, so it is a nice hike to take with the family.

Dogs are not allowed on the trail. Bathrooms are located near the trailhead, and GPS won't work in the park. Download a map before heading out.

Best time to visit: The trail is best used March through October. The trail does get busy, so go early.

Pass/permit/fees: It costs $25 to park at Joshua Tree State Park.

How to get there: Joshua Tree is accessible from either Interstate 10 or Highway 62.

What to Pack: Sunblock, sunglasses, a hat, plenty of water, and snacks like trail mix, jerky, and protein bars are great to bring on your hike.

What can you find? The area was used in the 1930s to mine gold, and there are plenty of historical markers along the trail that give a history of the mine. You can still spot an old windmill and the remains of the mill and mine. There are jackrabbits hopping around near the trail as well as desert flowers and blooming cacti.

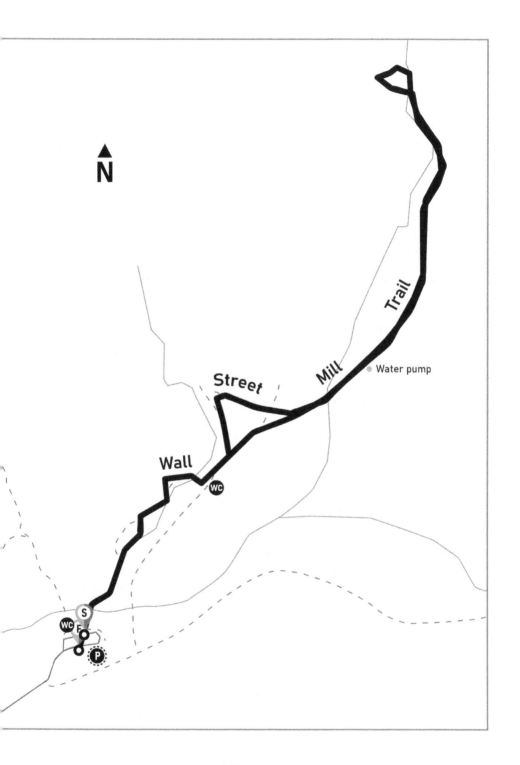

Cross Trail, Palm Desert

Cross Trail is a 2.3-mile out-and-back trail that can get difficult in certain spots with rocky steep terrain. It is best suited for younger kids to teenagers. It is located between Coachella Valley near Palm Springs. Dogs can use this trail but must be kept on a leash. Bathrooms are not located near the trailhead.

Best time to visit: The trail is accessible all year round but is best in the morning before it gets crowded.

Pass/permit/fees: Parking is free by the trailhead.

How to get there: The Cross Trail is located off of Interstate Highway 10. Use your GPS for more detailed directions off the interstate.

What to pack: There is no shade, so bring a hat, sunblock, and sunglasses. The terrain is dusty and rocky, so good hiking boots with ankle support are useful. Water is available at the trailhead, so make sure your water bottle is completely full for your hike. Bring light snacks for when you take a break at the end of the trail.

What can you find? The Cross Trail ends at a huge cross that is illuminated at night. The local church maintains the cross and sometimes ceremonies are held there. There are colorful rocks at the bottom of the cross where people leave their prayers and well wishes. Lots of chipmunks have been spotted on the trail.

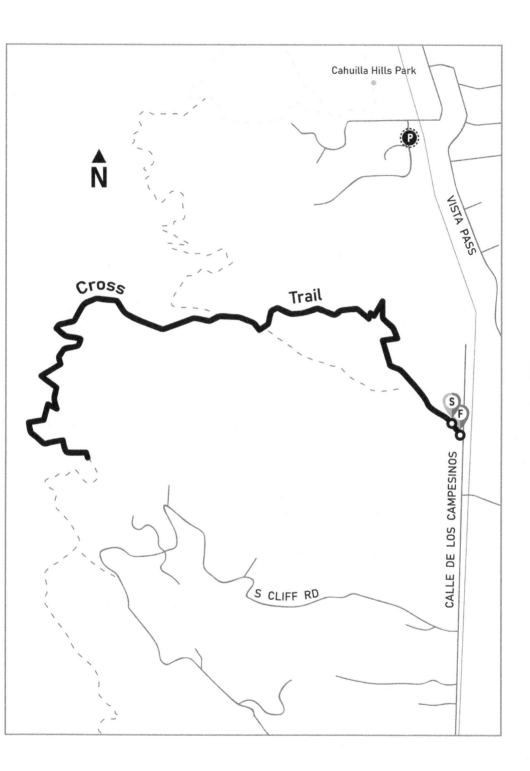

Bump and Grind Trail, Santa Rosa and San Jacinto Mountains National Monument

Bump and Grind is a 4-mile out-and-back hike. The trail can get steep and moderately difficult at times. It is best suited for younger kids to teenagers.

Dogs are not allowed on this trail and bathrooms are located in the shopping plaza.

Best time to visit: Bump and Grind is best May through January. The trail closes early in the year to prevent humans from interacting with the bighorn sheep in the spring. Go early as this trail gets very busy.

Pass/permit/fees: Parking is free on the road at the trailhead.

How to get there: Palm Desert is located off of State Highway 111 in Palm Desert, CA.

What to Pack: Make sure to pack plenty of water for the hike. Small snacks like trail mix and jerky are great, as are sandwiches that won't spoil. There is no shade, so bring sunblock, a hat, and sunglasses. Hiking shoes with good ankle support are great for the rocky terrain.

What can you find? There are lots of bighorn sheep that may be spotted during your hike. The trail is behind a shopping center with plenty of restaurants to eat at afterwards, and there is a living desert zoo in the same plaza.

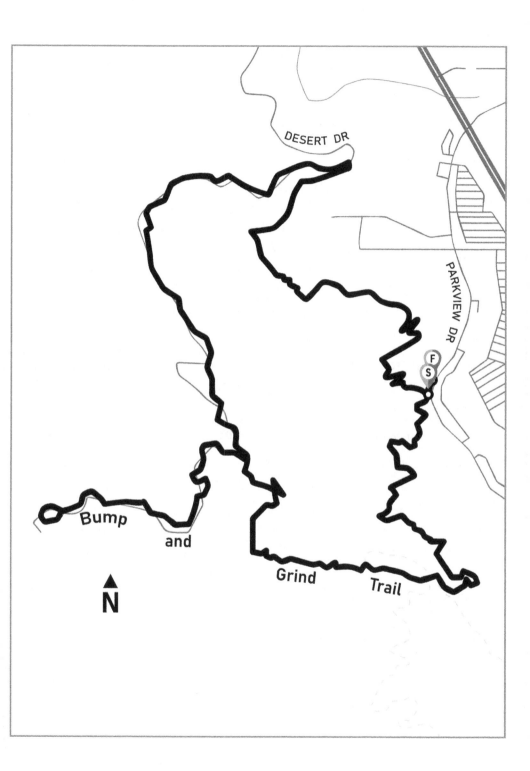

Ladder Canyon and Painted Canyon Trail, Santa Rosa and San Jacinto Mountains National Monument

Ladder Canyon and Painted Canyon Trail is a 4.4-mile loop trail that can get very rocky and steep. It is best suited for older kids and teenagers. You will climb several ladders to scale the walls of the canyons, so some scrambling may be in order to complete this hike. The trail head is at a very sandy location, so 4WD vehicles are best suited to access this trail.

Dogs are not allowed, and there are no bathrooms near the trail.

Best time to visit: The trail is best October through April. There is lots of traffic on this trail (one of the most popular in Southern California) so go early.

Pass/permit/fees: Parking is free at the trailhead.

How to get there: Palm Desert is located near Highway 111. Use your GPS for more detailed directions to the trailhead.

What to pack: Pack plenty of sunblock, a hat, and sunglasses. Sturdy hiking boots are a must, as there is a lot of climbing, sandy terrain, and rocks. Bring light snacks and plenty of water for this sometimes-strenuous hike.

What can you find? Aside from beautiful views, there are wildflowers and snakes along the trail. A lot of the rock formations were created by the San Andreas Fault. There are many slot canyons.

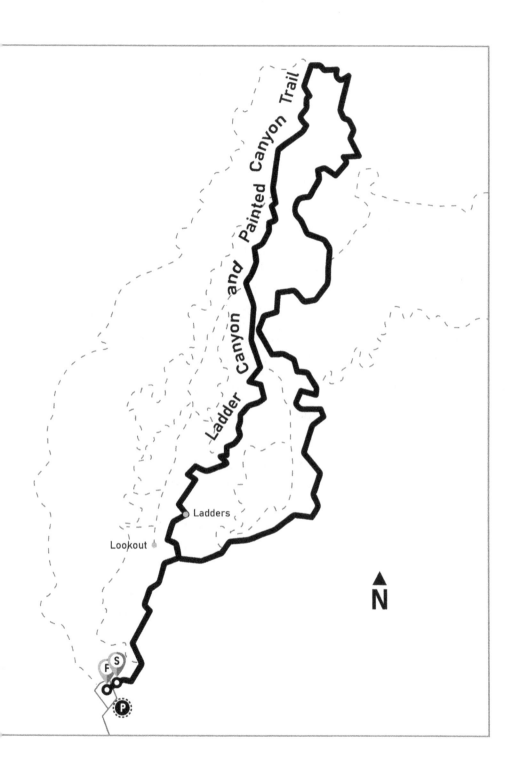

Ladder Canyon and Painted Canyon Trail

Ladders

Lookout

N

McGee Creek Canyon, Mammoth Lakes, CA

The Sierra Nevada Range is located in the most eastern part of California, running from the Mojave Desert all the way north to Oregon.

The McGee Creek Canyon Trail is a 3.6-mile hike that is located in Inyo National Forest. The trail is great for older kids to teenagers and gets moderately difficult. At certain times of the year, there will be snow on the ground. Dogs are allowed on this trail. Bathrooms are located at nearby campgrounds.

Best time to visit: The trail is best from May to September when there is not an abundant amount of snow on the ground.

Pass/permit/fees: It costs $5 to enter Inyo National Forest.

How to get there: Inyo National Forest is located on McGee Creek Road off Highway 395.

What to pack: For snow, make sure to have shoe spikes for safer hiking as well as hiking poles. Goggles and sunglasses keep blowing snow out of your eyes. A goose down jacket will keep you warm, as well as a hat and gloves. In warmer weather, pack sunblock, sunglasses, and a hat. Bring plenty of snacks and water for the hike.

What can you find? Horses are allowed on the trail. There are tons of wildflowers and trees like Jeffrey pines and bristlecone.

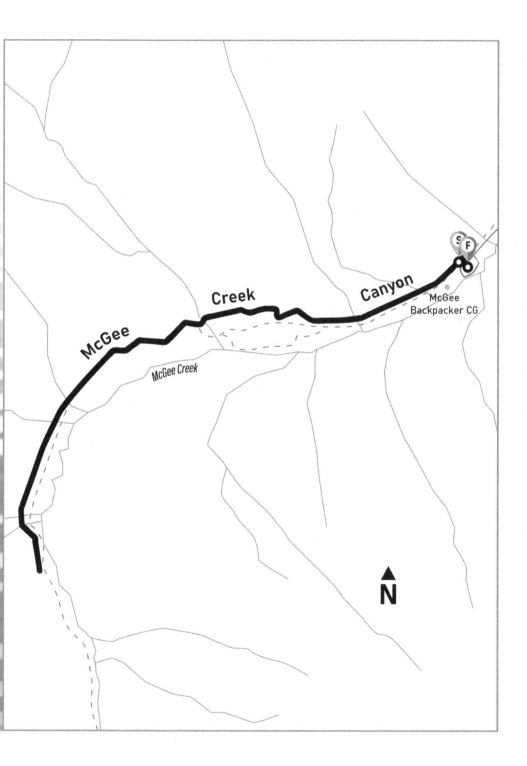

McGee

Creek

Canyon

McGee Creek

McGee
Backpacker CG

S F

N

Convict Lake, Inyo National Forest

Convict Lake is a 2.5-mile hike that is relatively flat, which is good for toddlers and younger kids. The trail goes out towards the lake and loops around.

Dogs are allowed on this trail, and bathrooms are located at a nearby campsite.

Best time to visit: The trail is best from June through November. Go early, as it gets crowded.

Pass/permit/fees: It costs $5 to enter Inyo National Forest.

How to get there: Inyo National Forest is located on McGee Creek Road off of Highway 395.

What to pack: Pack good shoes for the walk. Bring plenty of water and light snacks to pick on while you are walking. Bring a bathing suit for swimming in the lake. If the forecast calls for snow, pack your winter gear.

What can you find? Expect a lot of wildflowers, birds, and gorgeous views. In the summer, you can swim and fish in the lake.

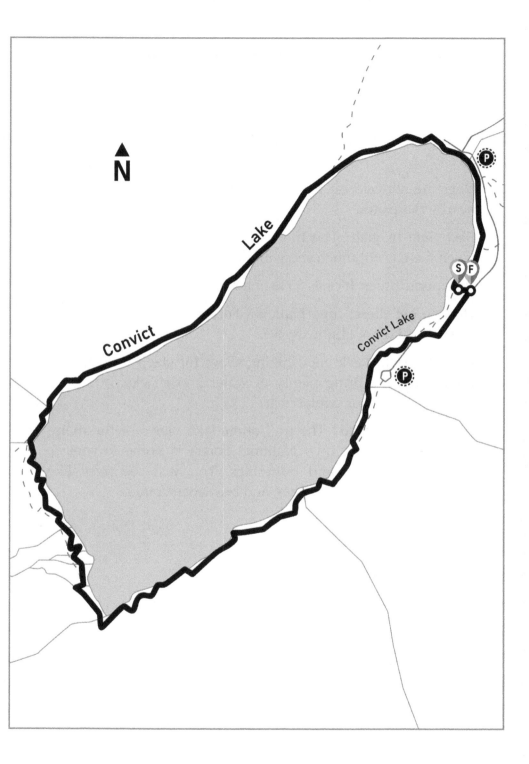

Fern Lake Trail, Inyo National Forest

Fern Lake Trail is a 3.1-mile out-and-back trail. It is great for younger kids to teenagers. The trail can get steep in certain areas.

Dogs are allowed on this trail, and bathrooms are located in nearby campsites.

Best time to visit: The trail is best from June to November when there is not much snow in the area.

Pass/permit/fees: It costs $5 to enter Inyo National Forest.

How to get there: Inyo National Forest is located on McGee Creek Road off of Highway 395.

What to pack: Pack good hiking shoes for steep inclines and uneven terrain. Bring plenty of water and snacks. In snowy weather, pack your winter gear.

What can you find? The trail offers lake views of the many lakes in the forest. Inyo National Forest is home to snakes, black bears, frogs, and butterflies. You will see trees like lodgepole pines, Jeffrey pines, and bristlecone pines.

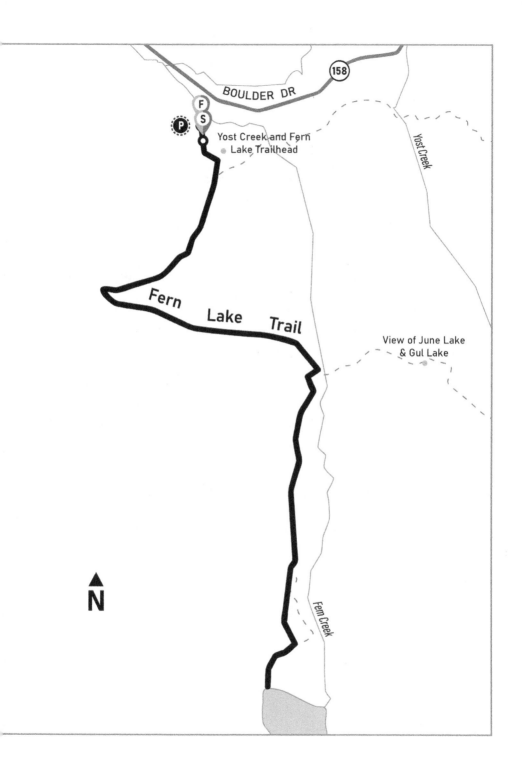

Agnew Lake and Gem Lake, Inyo National Forest

The Agnew Lake and Gem Lake Trail is a 4.4-mile hike for older kids to teenagers. Parts of the hike are very difficult and are not suited for beginner hikers.

Dogs are allowed on this trail while on a leash, and bathrooms are located at nearby campsites.

Best time to visit: The trail is best from April to September.

Pass/permit/fees: It is $5 to enter Inyo National Forest.

How to get there: Inyo National Forest is located on McGee Creek Road off of Highway 395.

What to pack: For this difficult hike, pack sturdy hiking shoes with great support. Hiking poles may be useful, as well as a lightweight backpack. Have sunblock, a hat, and sunglasses. Bring plenty of water and light snacks. Pack bug spray for mosquitos and be careful of ticks.

What can you find? This hike offers great views of the surrounding lakes including June Lake. There is an abundance of wildflowers, alpine trees, and mountain animals.

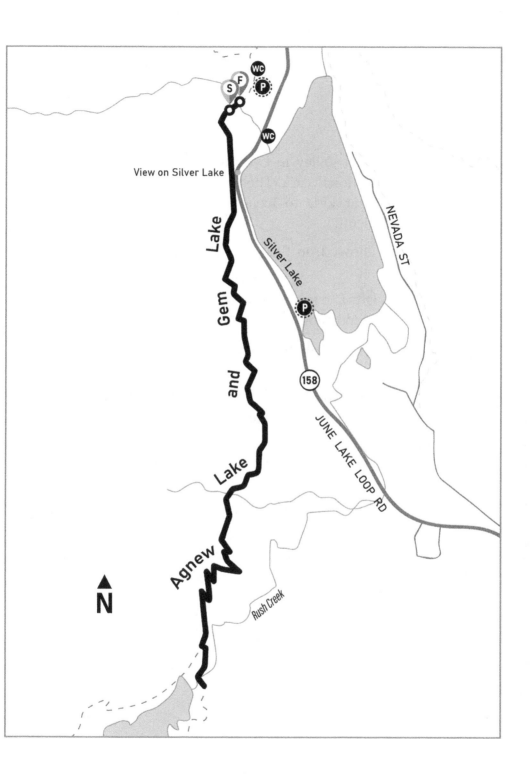

Condor Gulch Overlook, East Pinnacle National Park

East of the Salinas Valley in Central California, you will find East Pinnacle National Park. The trail is a 1.9-mile hike that is great for younger kids to teenagers. At times, it does get moderately difficult.

Dogs are not allowed on this trail. Bathrooms are located in parking areas.

Best time to visit: The trail is accessible all year round. There is less traffic in the morning.

Pass/permit/fees: It costs $30 to enter East Pinnacle National Park.

How to get there: The Condor Gulch Trail is located close to Highway 146, which is accessible via Highway 101.

What to pack: Bring plenty of water, sunblock, and a hat. Pack light snacks like trail mix and jerky. Good hiking boots are a good idea for the more difficult parts of the hike.

What can you find? Condor Gulch is a release for condors. You may spot some on your hike, along with turkey vultures, woodpeckers, and hawks. Wildflowers include California poppies, larkspurs, mariposa lilies, and California buckeye.

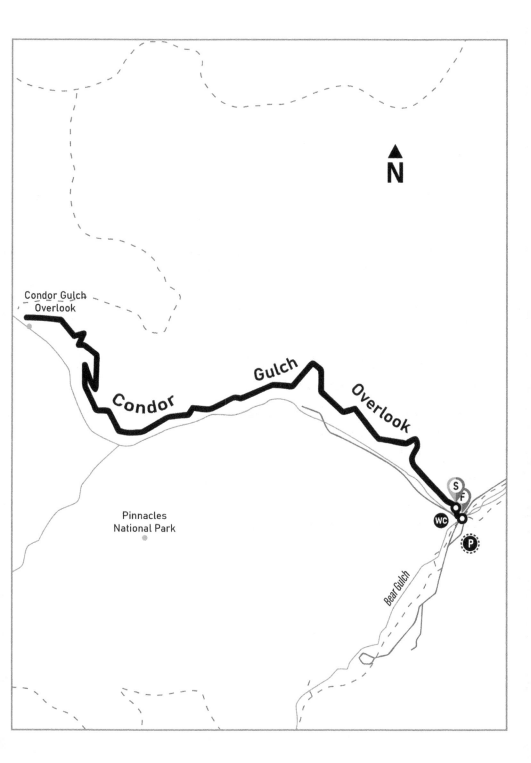

Moses Spring to Rim Trail, East Pinnacle National Park

Moses Spring to Rim Trail is a 2.5-mile hike that can get moderately difficult in spots. It is great for younger kids to teenagers.

Dogs are not permitted on the trail. Bathrooms are located in parking areas and campsites.

Best time to visit: The trail is accessible all year long but gets crowded on the weekends.

Pass/permit/fees: It costs $30 to enter East Pinnacle National Park.

How to get there: The trail is located near Highway 146, which is accessible from Highway 101.

What to pack: Pack plenty of water and snacks for the trail. Good hiking boots are great for the terrain of the trail. Also, bring a flashlight for the cave.

What can you find? There are plenty of lake views, as well as Bear Gulch Cave, which is great for kids to explore. The area has a unique terrain where a monolith has formed along the trail.

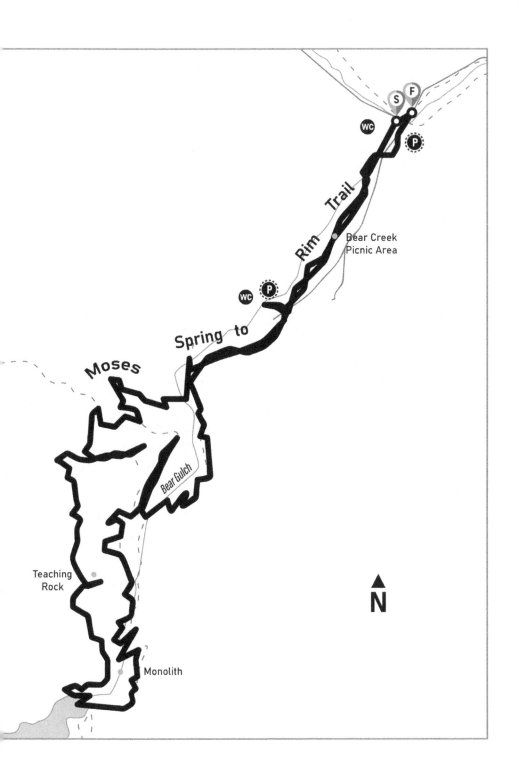

Chalone Peak Trail, East Pinnacle National Park

Chalone Peak Trail is a 7.7-mile hike that is good for teenagers. The trail is a gradual upward slope that makes it not too difficult. There is lots of wilderness to see on this hike. Chalone Peak is the highest point in all of Pinnacles National Park.

Dogs are not allowed on this trail. Bathrooms are located in parking areas and campsites.

Best time to visit: The trail is accessible all year round.

Pass/permit/fees: It costs $30 to enter East Pinnacle National Park.

How to get there: The trail is located near highway 146, which is accessible from Highway 101.

What to pack: Pack plenty of snacks and sandwiches for this long hike. Plenty of water is necessary. If your backpack has a bladder then use it. Sturdy hiking shoes as well as sunblock and sunglasses are a must.

What can you find? There are lots of wildflowers on the trail, as well as famous rock formations like The Sisters, The Love Handles, Ridge Rock, and the Hatchet. There is also a fire lookout tower on the trail that is no longer in use.

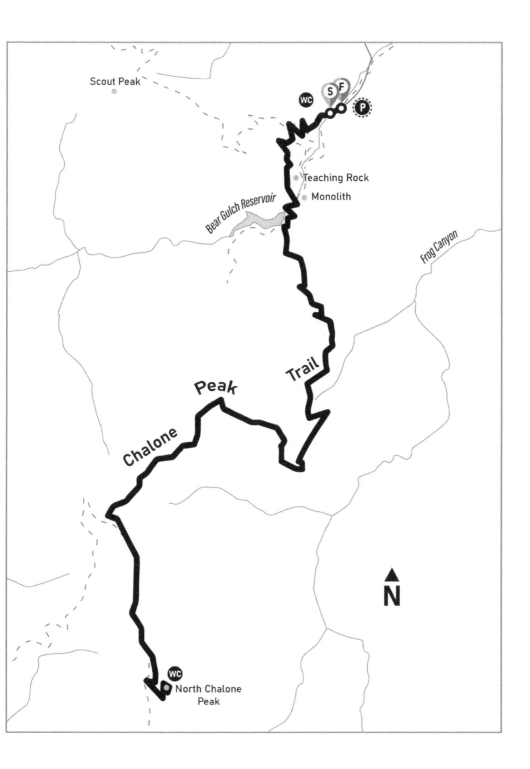

Scout Peak

WC S F P

Teaching Rock

Bear Gulch Reservoir

Monolith

Frog Canyon

Peak

Trail

Chalone

N

WC
North Chalone
Peak

High Peaks to Bear Gulch Loop, East Pinnacle National Park

This trail is a 7.7-mile hike that is best suited for teenagers. The trail can get difficult at times.

Dogs are not allowed on this trail. Bathrooms are located in parking areas and campsites.

Best time to visit: The trail is accessible all year round, but spring and fall are the best times to go. Arrive early, as parking at the trailhead is very limited.

Pass/permit/fees: It costs $30 to enter East Pinnacle National Park.

How to get there: Take Highway 146 to access the park, which is accessible from Highway 101.

What to pack: Pack good hiking gear like sturdy shoes with ankle support, hiking poles, and plenty of snacks and water. Bring sunblock, a hat, and sunglasses. Bring a flashlight for exploring the caves.

What can you find? The trail includes Bear Gulch Cave and Balconies Cave. You will also pass High Peak Monument, which was formed when the San Andreas Fault moved, causing a volcano to explode. There are plenty of wildflowers along the way, as well as condors, turkey vultures, and hawks.

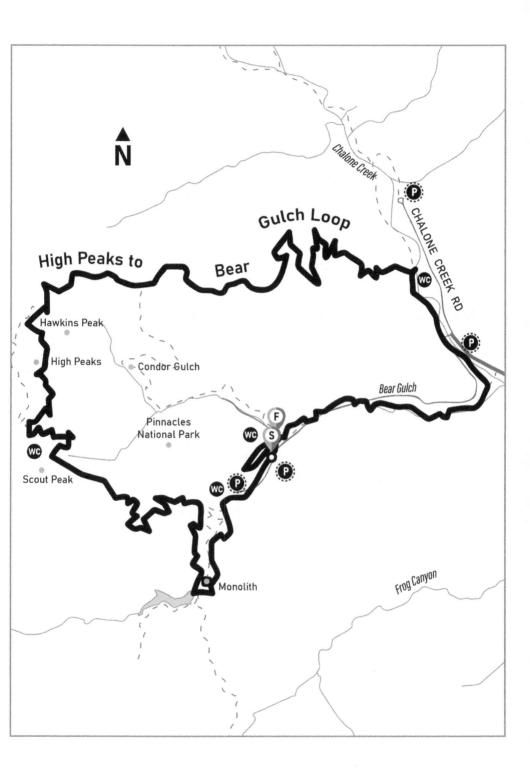

Prewett Point Trail, West Pinnacle National Park

The Prewett Point Trail is a short .7-mile trail that is best for toddlers and younger kids. The trail never gets too steep, allowing it to be on the easier side. This is also one of the newest trails in the park. The trail is stroller and wheelchair accessible.

Dogs are not allowed on the trail. Bathrooms are located at the trailhead at the visitor center.

Best time to visit: The trail is accessible all year round.

Pass/permit/fees: It costs $30 to enter Pinnacles National Forest.

How to get there: The trail head is on Highway 146, which is accessible from Highway 101.

What to pack: It can get sunny and hot, so pack plenty of sunblock, a hat, and sunglasses. Plenty of water is a must, as are good shoes for the walk.

What can you find? There are deer and turkeys on the trail at certain times. You will also see wildflowers and a view of Hain Wilderness.

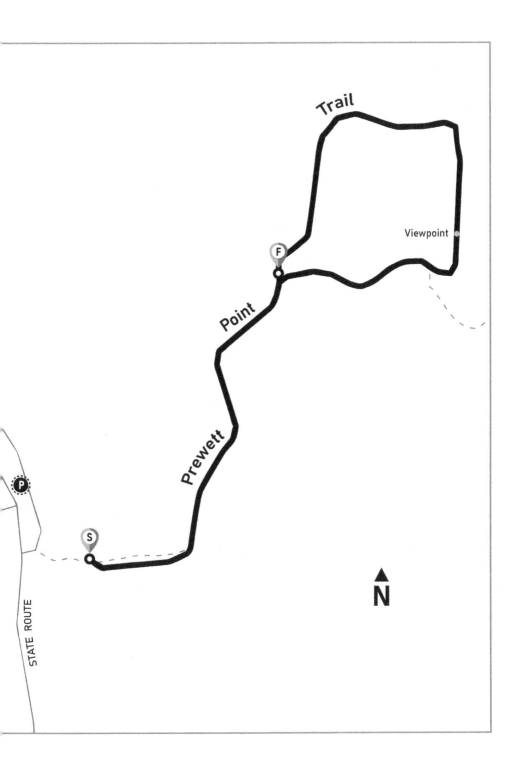

Trail

Viewpoint

Point

Prewett

P

S

F

STATE ROUTE

N

107

Jawbone Trail, West Pinnacle National Forest

One of the newer trails in the park, Jawbone Trail is a 1.4-mile hike that is great for toddlers and younger kids.

Dogs are not allowed on the trail, and the bathrooms are located at the trailhead at the visitor center.

Best time to visit: The trail is accessible all year round.

Pass/permit/fees: It costs $30 to enter West Pinnacle National Park.

How to get there: The trailhead is located at the visitor center on Highway 146, which is accessible from Highway 101.

What to pack: It can get very hot on the trail, so pack plenty of water, snacks, sunblock, a hat, and sunglasses. Good shoes are a must for the hike.

What can you find? There are deer and turkeys along the trail at certain times. You will see several types of wildflowers and views of the mountains and peaks.

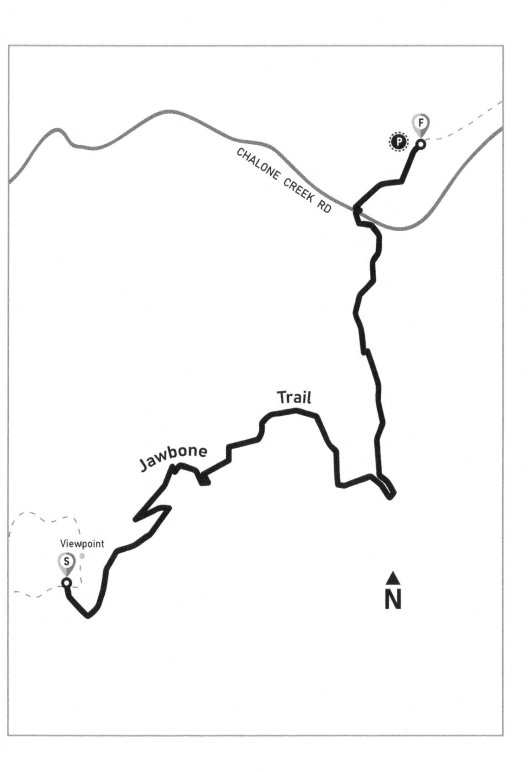

CHALONE CREEK RD

Trail

Jawbone

Viewpoint

S

F

P

N

There is so much more to see....

There is so much more to explore, but this is a great start.

For information on all of the national parks of California, visit: www.nps.gov. For information on the state parks of California visit: www.parks.ca.gov.

These sites will give you information on up-to-date entrance fees and how to purchase a park pass for unlimited access to national and state parks. These sites will also introduce you to all of the trails of each park.

Always check before you go to make sure there are no closures due to fires or extreme weather. Some trails close when there is heavy rain or snow in the area, and other parks close parts of their land for the migration of wildlife. Check the above websites for the most up to date information.

SAFETY FIRST!

It is always a great idea to pack a first aid kit before going on your hike. Cell phone service is spotty or sometimes not available in state and national parks, so staying safe and being able to find help is completely up to you. Make sure your kit is full of any bandages or creams you may need for burns, bleeding, or twists and sprains. Always have your wits about you and be observant. Know how to get to visitor centers for help. Always check this guide and the above sites for the wildlife in the area and be vigilant. NEVER approach wildlife. These animals are not domesticated and will use their survival instincts to attack. You may be unaware that wildlife is transporting their young, and they are very protective.

Enjoy your hikes, and take in the beauty that is the deserts, beaches, mountains, parks, valleys, and views of California. Happy Hiking!